THE NEW MERMAIDS

The Jew of Malta

MERCHANT - VENICE

THE NEW MERMAIDS

General Editors
PHILIP BROCKBANK
BRIAN MORRIS

The Jew of Malta

CHRISTOPHER MARLOWE

Edited by T. W. CRAIK

A New Mermaid

 A MERMAID DRAMABOOK
HILL AND WANG • NEW YORK
A DIVISION OF FARRAR, STRAUS AND GIROUX

Manufactured in the United States of America

34567890

CONTENTS

ACKNOWLEDGEMENTS

MY CHIEF DEBT is to H. S. Bennett's edition of *The Jew of Malta* (Methuen, 1931: Vol. III of *The Works and Life of Christopher Marlowe*, general editor R. H. Case). I have relied upon his full textual apparatus for the readings of previous editors, together with the edition of C. F. Tucker Brooke (Oxford, 1910). I have consulted the critical notes of A. Dyce (1850; 1858), H. Spencer (*Elizabethan Plays*, Heath, Boston, 1933) and H. S. Bennett. The editorial reading at I.i, 51 is from an article by J. C. Maxwell in the *Modern Language Review*, XLVIII, 1953. A list of recommended critical works precedes the text.

T. W. CRAIK

INTRODUCTION

THE AUTHOR

CHRISTOPHER MARLOWE was born at Canterbury in February 1564, the second of nine children. His family had lived there for several generations, and had been prosperous tradesmen; his father was a shoemaker, his grandfather and great-grandfather tanners. Marlowe's early education is not known, but when nearly fifteen he entered the King's School, Canterbury, and thence he went to Corpus Christi College, Cambridge, two years later. He obtained his B.A. in 1584, and his M.A. in 1587. During these three latter years he had frequently been absent from Cambridge, on secret government service (probably as a messenger or as a spy): government intervention was necessary before the university would grant his M.A. On leaving Cambridge he went to London, where *Tamburlaine* was shortly performed by the Lord Admiral's Men. The chronological order of his later plays is uncertain. He became not only a celebrated poet and playwright but a notorious freethinker and a reputed militant atheist; at the same time he seems to have continued in the secret service of the government. He was also involved in certain breaches of the peace; in one of these a man was killed (not by Marlowe), and Marlowe was imprisoned for twelve days before being released on bail, and later discharged. In May 1593 he was arrested on suspicion of dangerous religious opinions (Kyd the dramatist, himself in prison for suspected authorship of inflammatory propaganda against immigrants, had informed against him); he was not charged, but was required to report daily to the Privy Council. On 30th May he was stabbed in a tavern at Deptford, by one of three men with whom he had spent the day there, in a quarrel in which (according to their evidence at the inquest) Marlowe was the aggressor. It has been suggested that his death was contrived for political reasons, but there are no good grounds for rejecting the inquest evidence that the quarrel was about the tavern reckoning. His death was described by several contemporary moralists as the fitting end to a scandalous life.

THE PLAY

The date of *The Jew of Malta* is uncertain. It was not a new play when the theatre manager Philip Henslowe received fifty shillings at a performance by Lord·Strange's Men on 26th February 1592; yet it must have been written after the death of the Duke of Guise, mentioned in its prologue. This famous politician's assassination occurred on 23rd December 1588, and as the reference seems topical, the play can be assigned with reasonable confidence to 1589 or 1590. The chronology of Marlowe's plays being controversial, *The Jew of Malta* cannot be given a certain place in it, but the play is known to be later than *Tamburlaine* and earlier than *Edward II*, and is usually placed before *Dr. Faustus*.

No printed text exists before Nicholas Vavasour's quarto of 1633, though in 1594 the Stationers' Register records that Nicholas Ling and Thomas Millington were licensed to publish 'The famouse tragedie of the Riche Jewe of Malta' (evidently Marlowe's play, as the title is identical with that of the 1633 edition). Whether an edition of 1594 was printed and has wholly disappeared, or whether it was for some reason prevented, is unknown.

The long delay between the play's composition and the appearance of the first surviving text has raised the question of authenticity. The quarto of 1633 followed a recent revival of the play at Court and at a public theatre, the Cockpit. This revival was superintended by the dramatist Thomas Heywood, who furnished prologues and epilogues for both occasions, and there has been speculation as to whether Heywood tampered with the play, and whether it had suffered corruption during the previous forty years. Against the first possibility it may be objected that Heywood makes no claim to have altered the play, which he confesses is old and yet, he hopes, not unacceptable to the Court of Charles I; and, against the second, that though the text is carelessly printed (like that of many Elizabethan and Jacobean plays) it shows no sign of being a 'Bad Quarto' in the technical sense of the term, that is, one imperfectly reconstructed by memory or some other process.[1]

Attempts to trace revision or corruption of the text have resulted partly from the conviction that the play deteriorates sharply after its first two acts. It is true that long speeches expressing emotions and

[1] See J. C. Maxwell, 'How bad is the text of *The Jew of Malta?*' (*Modern Language Review*, XLVIII, 1953). Other important contributions to this discussion have been made by A. M. Clark, *Thomas Heywood* (1931); H. S. Bennett (editorial introduction), *The Jew of Malta* (1931); and F. S. Boas, *Christopher Marlowe* (1940).

purposes grow fewer, and that numerous events follow in rapid succession: there is 'the substitution of a technique of action for a technique of verse'.[1] It is not necessarily true, however, that this change represents revision or corruption destroying Marlowe's work, or Marlowe himself failing to carry through his original intention. As J. C. Maxwell says, 'it is hard to see these early scenes as pointing forward to anything substantially different from what we actually have'.[2] The 'cauldron for the Jew' was among the properties of the Admiral's Men (who had possessed the play since 1594) when an inventory was made in 1598; and Barabas's fate, and the career that led him to it, must have always formed part of *The Jew of Malta*. It is regrettable that not only the projected edition of 1594 fails to exist, but also 'a ballad intituled the murtherous life and terrible death of the riche jew of Malta', entered in the Stationers' Register at the same time to another printer: if this ballad survived, it would probably corroborate this conclusion.

This violent story has no known source. The device whereby Barabas causes one friar to strike down and supposedly kill the other friar's already dead body has counterparts in an English jest-book story and an Italian *novella*, but it is uncertain whether it was taken directly from either of these: it may have circulated by word of mouth.[3] For the rest, Marlowe has drawn mainly on his imagination, supplemented by his casual reading in recent works of history and geography. Barabas himself could have no historical original, but there were certain Jews who became important figures in Mediterranean politics, and their careers may have stimulated Marlowe's imagination: a Portuguese Jew called Miques settled in Constantinople about 1555, where he became confidential adviser to the Sultan and was made Duke of Naxos and the Cyclades; another Jew called Passi worked as a Turkish diplomat and spy. Marlowe could have read of Miques in a chronicle of 1584 which he is known to have used,[4] and he might hear of Passi during his own secret activities on the government's behalf. Malta was the headquarters of the Knights of St. John of Jerusalem from 1530 (they had been at Rhodes from 1310 to 1522, when it was captured by the Turks), and in 1565 had

[1] M. C. Bradbrook, *Themes and Conventions of Elizabethan Tragedy* (second edition, 1952), 158.
[2] 'The Plays of Christopher Marlowe', in *A Guide to English Literature, II: The Age of Shakespeare*, ed. B. Ford (1955).
[3] F. S. Boas, *Christopher Marlowe* (1940) gives details of these versions. He discusses also Fleay's theory (1891) that this episode is due to Heywood as reviser, Heywood having used the *novella* version twice before, in his play *The Captives* and also in a collection of prose stories about women (both 1624). Boas's comment is reasonable: 'Is it likely that Heywood, having thus twice made use of the whole story, would nine years afterwards drag its central incident into *The Jew of Malta?*'
[4] H. S. Bennett, in his edition (p. 10), cites an article by Ethel Seaton.

successfully withstood a Turkish siege: the Turkish general was called Selim, not Selim-Calymath (but Marlowe always preferred proper names which were polysyllabic). Reading a description of Malta in Nicholas Nicholay's *Navigations, Peregrinations and Voyages made into Turkey* (translated from the French in 1585), he might read on to the siege of Tripoli, where a spy showed the invading Turks that the city's weakest point was 'against the governor's lodging ... standing towards the ditch' (*cf.* V.i, 87–95); and in another description of this siege of Tripoli, in De Villegagnon's *Discours de la Guerre de Malte* (1553) he might find the name Fernese (Ferneze) which he gives his Governor.[1]

Marlowe's historical reading, then, gave him the political framework of his story; but only the framework, not the substance of the story itself, as in *Tamburlaine, Edward II*, or his play about contemporary French politics, *The Massacre at Paris*. The substance of *The Jew of Malta* is the wholly personal conflict between Barabas and the other characters, principally the Governor, with whom he is at enmity.

In inventing his own plot, Marlowe followed the example of Kyd, whose *Spanish Tragedy* (first printed in 1592) is the prototype of Elizabethan and Jacobean revenge tragedy. The violent actions and the complicated intrigue of Kyd's play provoke excitement and suspense. The hero Hieronimo's problems are purely practical ones: to detect his son's murderers, to contrive an ingenious revenge upon them, and to conceal his discoveries and intentions until he is ready to act (so that his enemies do not act first). To do all this requires a cool head and a resolute spirit, and these qualities, together with the pathos of his situation, made old Hieronimo an impressive part for Edward Alleyn, the brilliant young actor who also performed Marlowe's Barabas. In the later scenes, Hieronimo develops a sinister irony, assuring the murderers that the drama he is inviting them to take part in with him will prove 'wondrous plausible' (it is to end in all their deaths), and that they need not disdain to act, because 'Nero thought it no disparagement'. At the last, his revenge accomplished, he glories in his enemies' deaths and crowns the action with a stoical suicide.

The revenger's enemies too are intriguers (just as in *Hamlet* we have the plots and counterplots of Hamlet and the King), and one of them, Lorenzo, is the first 'machiavellian villain' of the Elizabethan stage, the first of a line of unscrupulous egoists who justify their dissimulation and double-dealing by self-interest, the only end that they recognize: '*Ego mihimet sum semper proximus*' (*The Jew of Malta*, I.i, 192). Lorenzo, for example, thus rids himself of his two sub-

[1] See J. Bakeless, *The Tragicall History of Christopher Marlowe* (1942), I, 334–345, on these books.

ordinates who have assisted in murdering Hieronimo's son: he hires one of them to shoot the other, promising him a pardon at the gallows, but withholds the pardon, so that his tool and dupe goes confidently to his death. The King's ambiguous death-warrant sent by Young Mortimer in Marlowe's *Edward II*, Edmund's forged letter and the use he makes of it in *King Lear*, and the secret document which Claudius sends with Hamlet to England, are (like the double forged challenge in *The Jew of Malta*) characteristic instruments of the 'sound Machevill' (*The Jew of Malta*, Heywood's prologue spoken at Court, line 8).

The Jew of Malta resembles *The Spanish Tragedy* in its sensationalism of plot and its emphasis on contrivance and villainy. It is, however, a more ambiguous, equivocal play. Whereas the revenger of *The Spanish Tragedy* is the hero and commands our entire sympathy in the 'wild justice' of his actions, Marlowe's Jew is a villain, yet a villain who can (at the beginning, at least) make out a kind of moral case for himself by pointing to the duplicity of his enemies, and who can arouse our enthusiasm and glee by his zestful pursuit of ends which we fully recognize as villainous.

Given such a plot, and such a character at its centre, two related questions arise. First, what is the theme of the play? Is it Barabas's villainous career, or is it universal machiavellism? And second, what is the prevailing spirit of the play? It is described on its title-page, and again in Marlowe's prologue, as a tragedy, yet it contains much that seems deliberately comic and grotesque.

These questions are incapable of simple, definite answers. Guidance may, however, be sought first in the prologue of Machevill (Machiavelli, in his Elizabethan guise as sponsor of 'politic' villainy). Marlowe's prologues, though they cannot be comprehensive, are reliable statements of what the plays contain: this one establishes that 'machiavellism' is widespread, even among those who openly repudiate it, and that the Jew whose tragedy is presented is in general terms a machiavellian (whose 'money was not got without my means'). Barabas himself, embarking on his spectacular crimes and engaging Ithamore as his instrument, gives him a much more particular account of his career (II.iii, 178–202). We ought not, perhaps, to attribute too much importance to these revelations: their essential dramatic purpose is to give Barabas a past sufficiently villainous to suit his present and his future, and to introduce a matching confession or boast from Ithamore; but they also serve to correct (as the prologue should forestall) the wrong inference that the Jew has been turned into a monster by the Christians' injustice. This injustice, to be sure, gives him the grounds for his revenge, but he was selfish and deceitful before his wealth was thus confiscated. His career, within the play, opens with self-confidence and self-sufficiency; proceeds to double-dealing (with the other Jews); then develops, through the cunning recovery of the money in his house (cunning with which we can feel some faint moral sympathy, since it immediately follows his dispossession, and since the innocent Abigail is his accomplice), to the cunning revenge on the Governor by exploiting the rivalry of Lodowick and Mathias (cunning with which, since it costs Abigail her whole happiness, we can feel no moral sympathy at all); and so culminates in the ruthless removal of all who know of his crimes, the double treachery during and after the Turkish siege, and the poetically just death in his own cauldron.

An Elizabethan dramatist, writing a sensational play on these doings, might have been content to make the villain the only schemer. Not so Marlowe. Far from trying to whitewash the Governor, he draws attention to his sharp practice in confiscating the tribute-money from the Jews, and to his sanctimonious justification of it. In later scenes, the Governor is an opportunist, when he is inspired by Del Bosco to convert the tribute-money into armaments, and when he double-crosses Barabas at the end. We must not, of course, forget that the Governor is partly an instrument of the plot (no confiscation, no revenge; no war, no treachery; no double-crossing, no poetic justice), and except where Marlowe dwells on his duplicity of motive we are hardly justified in arguing it from his actions. Even so, the Governor's brisk conclusion, when Barabas is dead and the Turks are in his hands, may be taken ironically:

> So march away, and let due praise be given
> Neither to fate nor fortune, but to heaven.

Heaven, it is clear, has helped those who have helped themselves. As for the Friars, their rivalry in blackmailing Barabas puts them on the moral level of Ithamore and Pilia-Borza, and we see their deaths with as little compunction. Marlowe takes a low view of friars and nuns, and cracks the stock Elizabethan–Protestant jokes about them ('Ay, and a virgin too, that grieves me most'). It is worth remembering that the Christians in the play, being all Catholics,[1] have no auto-matic claim on the sympathy of Marlowe's audience, though that audience was perfectly ready to suspend its prejudice when a good friar (like Friar Laurence in *Romeo and Juliet*) was wanted in a story. Even within *The Jew of Malta* there is not consistent hostility, and Abigail is not felt to be deceived in embracing the 'zealous ad-monition' of the Abbess when for the second time (and for very different reasons) she enters the nunnery as a refuge against the evil and cruelty of the world. Abigail is, in fact, the only character on

---

[1] Martin Del Bosco, for instance, announces himself as 'Vice-admiral unto the Catholic king' [of Spain]. The Armada (1588) was an event of very recent history.

whom Marlowe bestows the slightest real sympathy. No doubt the conception of Barabas as the central character – the self-assured engineer, the villain who so engagingly takes us into his confidence – has helped to exclude a full or sympathetic treatment of the other characters by the dramatist: our relation to Barabas, as he claims his victims, is more like our relation to Richard III than our relation to Iago. If we strongly supported the Christians we should not feel for Barabas the mingled attraction and repulsion that we do.

In any case, Marlowe probably felt little temptation to side firmly with the Christians against the Jew. From what his contemporaries tell us of his opinions, and from the evidence of his plays themselves, it seems that he had an open mind on most subjects (open to the point of inconsistency), a sceptical tendency which made him always able and willing to see two sides to every question, and a spirit which, like Iago's, was 'nothing if not critical'. He had already gone out of his way to introduce into *Tamburlaine, Part II*, an episode in which Christian leaders broke faith with their heathen enemies, who thereupon indignantly called on Christ for victory, and received it. In *The Jew of Malta* he several times toys with the idea that Christian belief and Christian practice do not necessarily go together: Barabas, in the first scene, reflects that he

> can see no fruits in all their faith,
> But malice, falsehood, and excessive pride,
> Which methinks fits not their profession.

The provocative tone of this remark, while certainly the speaker's, may be the dramatist's too. Likewise, reasoning with his reluctant daughter, Barabas expresses the unorthodox view that religious truth is relative:

> It's no sin to deceive a Christian;
> For they themselves hold it a principle,
> Faith is not to be held with heretics;
> But all are heretics that are not Jews;
> This follows well, and therefore daughter fear not.[1]
>   (II.iii, 313–17)

Marlowe, then, may have used his play to stir up and unsettle some conventional opinions of his time. This element, however, forms no great proportion of the whole play.[2]

---

[1] On the other hand, Marlowe seems to burlesque this argument when Ithamore paradoxically asserts, 'To undo a Jew is charity, and not sin' (IV.iv, 76) – a remark which may also refer back to the Governor's sanctimonious statement of his motives in confiscating Barabas's goods.

[2] This is not to discount an important article by G. K. Hunter ('The Theology of *The Jew of Malta*', *Journal of the Warburg and Courtauld Institutes*, XXVII, 1964, pp. 211–40), who shows how the traditional theological view

The play is essentially neither propagandist nor moralistic (in either an orthodox or an unorthodox spirit), but dramatic. Moral questions are not seriously discussed: they are ironically touched upon and left. If moral questions were an important element, the play's interest might be expected to reside as much in the characters as in the plot, but it does not. After his presentation (that is, up to and including his argument with the Governor about the tribute-money), even Barabas's character is expressed rather through what he does than through what he thinks: his intrigues, his ready response to each fresh challenge, the skill with which he plays his dangerous game (and a game it is to him, high though the stakes are) – these are the things which capture our interest. The manner of his contest with the Christians is more important than such moral basis as this contest may have.

Plot is more important than anything else in *The Jew of Malta*: Barabas's own character is itself important largely because of his vitality, his energy, in contriving and superintending this forward-driving action. The action, in its rapidity, continually flouts all verisimilitude to an extent which is striking even by Elizabethan conventions of construction. Letters are delivered when there has been no time to write them; the officers who, within half a line, fetch Barabas and Ithamore from two different places move faster than Ariel or Puck; and whenever a character is looked for, he is sure to be just walking in. The motivation, even that of the chief character, rather keeps pace with the action than governs it. When Barabas decides to betray the Turks to the Governor – having just betrayed the Governor to the Turks – he is given a soliloquy which explains his reasons. Marlowe seems not to care that the explanation is utterly unconvincing (Will Barabas's life be any less in danger if he trusts the Governor's word? Would Barabas trust anybody's word?): his concern is merely to provide sufficient explanation to usher in the climax of his play. Likewise, by dramatic sleight-of-hand, he persuades us (especially in the theatre) that events follow inevitably from actions which not even the most optimistic schemer could expect to produce them in reality. The 'fatal' blow which the first Friar deals to the second (suppose he had *kicked* him), and the coincidentally mutual stabbing of the rival suitors, are instances.[1]

---

[1] And conversely, there is little probability that Barabas's plan of poisoning Ithamore and his accomplices would miscarry through his being too sparing with the poison – especially after we have seen how efficiently and comprehensively he poisoned the nuns.

---

of Jews underlies the ideas ventilated in Marlowe's play, and how the 'degree of sympathy and admiration that Barabas is capable of exciting' is 'a counterpoint over a secure bass line of theological condemnation'. Particular allusions noted by Hunter are given in the critical notes.

These possible improbabilities are, however, consistent with the spirit of the whole play: paradoxically, their very frequency increases their dramatic plausibility. We accept them because of Ithamore's confidence in his master, and Barabas's confidence in himself. The mutual stabbing is particularly acceptable in the theatre because of Barabas's entry 'above', brooding gleefully over his handiwork, dominating the young men as their evil genius, *willing* them to kill each other. To ask where Barabas is supposedly standing would be idle, and to justify his presence by saying that he is on his own balcony (*cf.* II.iii, 183) would be idler still: he is simply occupying what is, in the circumstances, his most effective stage position.

It has already been said that Barabas's stratagem for removing Lodowick and Mathias commands no moral sympathy. It is, however, impossible not to relish his enjoyment of his success:

> So, now they have showed themselves to be tall fellows.
> [VOICES] (*within*) Part 'em, part 'em.
> BARABAS
> Ay, part 'em now they are dead. Farewell, farewell.
>
> (III.ii, 8–10)

That 'Farewell, farewell' is apparently a direct address to the audience,[1] delivered with all the assurance of the frank villain. We gasp at his effrontery, shake our fist at his villainy – and laugh at his gusto. Such spirited jocular wickedness had been a characteristic of the Vice in the moral interludes written before the public theatres were built. The plotting of the Vice had, however, been elementary, usually going no further than raising false hopes in his victim or deluding him by assuming a disguise and a virtue's name.[2] With the arrival of the machiavellian villain, the opportunities of developing this sinister jocularity were much increased: the bustling villainy of Richard III became possible, and so did his hypocrisy. Barabas is himself an accomplished hypocrite from the first:

> The man that dealeth righteously shall live:
> And which of you can charge me otherwise?
>
> (I.ii, 119–20)

This protestation is countered by the Governor's reply and has been nullified in advance by Machevill's prologue. In this scene of the tribute-money, Barabas plays the injured innocent as long as he has an audience, whether of Christians or Jews, and reserves his real

---

[1] Alternatively it may be taken as an apostrophe to the approaching citizens, or even as being bestowed (one 'farewell' each) on the corpses. But in all three cases, the tone of chuckling villainy is the same.
[2] For example, Nichol Newfangle in *Like Will to Like* (U. Fulwell, *c.* 1568) and Covetous in *Enough is as Good as a Feast* (W. Wager, *c.* 1564).

feelings and projects until he is alone. In the later scenes, having gained Ithamore as a confidant, he is able to dramatize his hypocrisy in such a way as to convince his dupes of his sincerity and to delight Ithamore with his duplicity. When he is offering to join the Friars, he heaps up images of self-mortification, to the accompaniment of Ithamore's admiring imitation which underlines (for the audience) his master's intentional dramatic irony:

> Would penance serve to atone for this my sin,
> I could afford to whip myself to death.
> ITHAMORE
> And so could I; but penance will not serve.
> BARABAS
> To fast, to pray, and wear a shirt of hair,
> And on my knees creep to Jerusalem . . .
>
> (IV.i, 58–62)

Later, having murdered one Friar and fixed the guilt on the other, he can protest sanctimoniously

> When shall you see a Jew commit the like?
> (IV.i, 194)

One sees his wink to Ithamore, which includes the audience too, as clearly as if it were a stage-direction; and Ithamore again underlines the dramatic irony (we have just seen this Jew commit the deed itself, with his Turkish slave's assistance):

> Why a Turk could ha' done no more.

Barabas can be unconsciously comic as well as consciously so. His appearance is grotesque as well as sinister: a contemporary allusion to the 'artificial Jew of Malta's nose'[1] is reinforced by Ithamore's casual tributes to its size and shape. Like Richard III and the morality Devil, Barabas has an ugly appearance to suit his character.[2] When he poisons the nuns' porridge, uttering a deadly curse upon his daughter, Ithamore gives a cheerful commentary, and adds to the comedy by his farcical promptitude to take the pot away before it is ready. Ithamore is, indeed, useful in varying the humour, which might otherwise depend too continually upon Barabas's conscious irony. As a blackmailer, he brings out the fact that Barabas is comic in adversity as well as in prosperity. The Jew's scene with Pilia-Borza (Ithamore's emissary) is a spirited confrontation of villain and rogue, with Barabas in actual retreat in spite of his private verbal triumphs; and the scene in which Barabas,

---

[1] By William Rowley, in *The Search for Money*, 1609.
[2] The Devil in the moral interludes wore a large misshapen nose, to which the Vice refers: I have given instances in *The Tudor Interlude* (1958).

disguised as a French musician, has to swallow down Ithamore's slanderous inventions, is even livelier. This latter scene is excellent when well acted: Barabas's sarcastic asides upon Pilia-Borza's comments, and his scandalized asides upon Ithamore's, are rapped out as he goes on smoothly playing his lute.

The aside is a prominent feature of the play's style: it harmonizes with the prominence of dramatic irony in the plot and of machiavellian cunning in the chief character; by keeping the audience constantly in touch with the villain, it assists the ambiguous response to his self-applauding immorality. In Ithamore's mouth, asides draw attention to the exaggerated violence of Barabas's curse when poisoning the porridge: colloquial prose impinges upon declamatory verse (as, in the opening scene of *Edward II*, the King's defiance of the Barons is applauded by the concealed Gaveston's 'Well done, Ned'). Ithamore is servant, confidant, foil and parodist. His doggerel raptures addressed to the Courtesan parody romantic verse: Faustus's words to Helen,

> I will be Paris, and for love of thee
> Instead of Troy shall Wittenberg be sacked,

have their burlesque counterpart in

> I'll be thy Jason, thou my golden fleece,

and Ithamore's tribute comes to a climax by plagiarizing Marlowe's own lyrical poem 'Come live with me and be my love' (see IV.ii, 96, and note).

Marlowe writes fewer long speeches in this play than he does in *Tamburlaine* or *Dr. Faustus*, where the long speech is the rule, not the exception. Such long speeches as he has, moreover, contain undertones which bear critically on the speaker, and anticipate (as was noted by T. S. Eliot) the method of Jonson. In his opening soliloquy, for example, Barabas declares that a single one of his precious stones

> May serve in peril of calamity
> To ransom great kings from captivity,

when he will later refuse to contribute to his country's tribute-money; he holds his daughter as dear, he says,

> As Agamemnon did his Iphigen;

yet he will sacrifice Abigail's happiness to his revenge, and will finally take her life not in pity but in anger. Again, arriving at midnight before the nunnery walls (II.i), he expresses his grief by comparing himself to

> the sad presaging raven that tolls
> The sick man's passport in her hollow beak;

but when Abigail throws down the gold to him, his mood changes with an extravagant swiftness reflected in his conscious change of imagery, from night to day, and from the raven to

> the morning lark,
> That I may hover with her in the air,
> Singing o'er these, as she does o'er her young

– and he breaks into Spanish exclamations. The stage direction here, 'Hugs his bags', further detracts from his stature: he is the 'bottle-nosed' Jew, the stage miser, hugging his money-bags as though they, and not Abigail, were his child.

This critical detachment, and the prominence of comedy throughout the play, do not prevent its being a 'tragedy'. The fall of a great villain made a satisfactory tragedy to the Elizabethans, if not to Aristotle—

> When the bad bleed, then is the tragedy good,

as the hero of *The Revenger's Tragedy* was later to remark of his own handiwork – and the literal fall of Barabas into his own cauldron makes a suitably spectacular end to a sensational play. *The Jew of Malta* is essentially a play for the theatre, and it is in the theatre that it must be judged, not according to preconceived notions of tragic dignity and tragic depth. It is not a profound play, but it is a good one, vigorous and varied in its dramatic effects, by no means appealing only to an unsophisticated audience (it deserved its double revival at Court and at the Cockpit), and not limited in its interest to its own age.

NOTE ON THE TEXT

The only extant text of *The Jew of Malta* is that of 1633, the Quarto published by Nicholas Vavasour, of which I have used the British Museum copy Ashley 1097. It is divided into acts (numbered in Latin) but not into scenes, and these have been supplied in the present edition. The spelling has been modernized, but punctuation usually follows the original.

Some speech-headings have been regularized. Thus, for example, the character who has hitherto been the first Friar is named by the Quarto as *Jacomo* (text *Iocoma*) throughout his last appearance.[1] I have continued to head his speeches *1 Friar*, preferring this to the usual editorial procedure of regularizing retrospectively and calling him *Jacomo* throughout, and his companion *Barnardine*, a distinction which seems to impose more personality on them than the nature of the play makes desirable. For the same reason I have preserved the naming *Governor* (not *Ferneze*), *Courtesan* (not *Bellamira*), and *Mother* (not *Katherine*: translating the *Mater* of the Quarto). All these characters are named according to their function. This throws into proper relief the naming of Barabas, Abigail, and Ithamore; Lodowick and Mathias; the Turkish Calymath and the Spanish Del Bosco; and Pilia-Borza, whose name (purse-stealer, pickpurse) defines his trade.

The Quarto is somewhat carelessly printed, with a number of trivial errors besides the more important and interesting ones recorded in the footnotes. The two quotations from Spanish in II.i were unintelligible to the printer, who set up unintelligible lines of his own in their place. He also had difficulty with proper names (*Abigail* is usually *Abigal* or *Abigall*; *Ithamore* usually *Ithimore* and once *Ithimer*; *Jacomo* and *Barnardine* are variously spelled; and *Pilia-Borza* once appears in the text itself as plain *Pilia*), which may imply that in his copy they were often represented by abbreviations. This, with the possibility that at V.iii, 5 he misplaced a line added marginally, suggests that he was not working from a fair copy but from a playhouse manuscript. His frequently setting up prose as verse (i.e. in lines roughly of verse length each beginning with a capital letter), and, less often, verse as prose, perhaps reinforces this conclusion. There are also places where evident mislining of verse occurs. I have rectified all these errors of lineation without indicating them in footnotes, but I have not allowed myself to be tempted to

[1] He is once earlier named, by Abigail at III.iii, 69.

emend for the sake of regularizing the metre, as some editors, notably
A. Wagner (1889), have done.

The play makes much use of 'aside' speeches and lines, and many
of Barabas's are indicated by italics as well as by the direction *aside*.
However, as italics are not used for the asides of other characters,
nor consistently for those of Barabas, I have not adopted this typo-
graphical convention, but have used the direction *aside* where it was
printed, and supplied it where it was not. All editorial additions,
except those recorded in the footnotes, are enclosed in square
brackets.

FURTHER READING

Bakeless, J. *The Tragicall History of Christopher Marlowe* (1942)

Bevington, D. M. *From 'Mankind' to Marlowe* (1962)

Boas, F. S. *Christopher Marlowe* (1940)

Bradbrook, M. C. *Themes and Conventions of Elizabethan Tragedy* (1935); second edition (1952)

Cole, D. *Suffering and Evil in the Plays of Christopher Marlowe* (1962)

Eliot, T. S. *Selected Essays* (1932) ('Christopher Marlowe')

Ellis-Fermor, U. M. *Christopher Marlowe* (1927)

Henderson, P. *Marlowe* (1952)

Kocher, P. H. *Christopher Marlowe* (1946)

Levin, H. *The Overreacher* (1952)

Maxwell, J. C. 'The Plays of Christopher Marlowe', in *A Guide to English Literature, II: The Age of Shakespeare*, ed. B. Ford (1955)

Poirier, M. *Christopher Marlowe* (1951)

Steane, J. B. *Marlowe* (1964)

Wilson, F. P. *Marlowe and the Early Shakespeare* (1953)

The Famous

TRAGEDY

OF

THE RICH IEVV

OF *MALTA*.

AS IT VVAS PLAYD

BEFORE THE KING AND

QVEENE, IN HIS MAJESTIES
Theatre at *White-Hall,* by her Majefties
Servants at the *Cock-pit*.

Written by CHRISTOPHER MARLO.

LONDON;
Printed by *I. B.* for *Nicholas Vavafour,* and are to be fold
at his Shop in the Inner-Temple, neere the
Church. 1633.

THE EPISTLE DEDICATORY

To my worthy friend Mr. THOMAS HAMMON,
of Gray's Inn, &c.

This play, composed by so worthy an author as Mr. Marlo; and
the part of the Jew presented by so unimitable an actor as Mr.
Allin, being in this later age commended to the stage: as I
ushered it unto the Court, and presented it to the Cock-pit,
with these Prologues and Epilogues here inserted, so now being   5
newly brought to the press, I was loath it should be published
without the ornament of an Epistle; making choice of you unto
whom to devote it; than whom (of all those gentlemen and ac-
quaintance, within the compass of my long knowledge) there
is none more able to tax ignorance, or attribute right to merit.   10
Sir, you have been pleased to grace some of mine own works
with your courteous patronage; I hope this will not be the worse
accepted, because commended by me; over whom, none can
claim more power or privilege than yourself. I had no better
New-Year's gift to present you with; receive it therefore as a   15
continuance of that inviolable obligement, by which he rests
still engaged; who as he ever hath, shall always remain,

Tuissimus:
THO. HEYWOOD.

3 *Allin* Edward Alleyn (1566–1626), acting *c.* 1583–1605
4 *the Court* the royal palace of Whitehall, London
  the Cock-pit a theatre in Drury Lane, London
10 *tax* censure
18 *tuissimus* (Latin) wholly yours

THE PROLOGUE SPOKEN AT COURT

Gracious and great, that we so boldly dare
('Mongst other plays that now in fashion are)
To present this; writ many years agone,
And in that age, thought second unto none;
We humbly crave your pardon: we pursue   5
The story of a rich and famous Jew
Who lived in Malta: you shall find him still,
In all his projects, a sound Machevill;
And that's his character: he that hath past
So many censures, is now come at last   10
To have your princely ears; grace you him; then
You crown the action, and renown the pen.

EPILOGUE

It is our fear (dread Sovereign) we have bin
Too tedious; neither can 't be less than sin
To wrong your princely patience: if we have,
(Thus low dejected) we your pardon crave:
And if aught here offend your ear or sight,   5
We only act, and speak, what others write.

Prologue
   8 *sound* complete
   9–10 *hath past/So many censures* has been so often judged
Epilogue
   4 *dejected* prostrated, bowing

4

THE PROLOGUE TO THE STAGE, AT THE COCK-PIT

We know not how our play may pass this stage,
But by the best of *poets in that age   *Marlo.
The Malta Jew had being, and was made;
And he, then by the best of †actors played: †Allin.
In *Hero and Leander*, one did gain   5
A lasting memory: in *Tamburlaine*,
This *Jew*, with others many, th'other wan
The attribute of peerless, being a man
Whom we may rank with (doing no one wrong)
Proteus for shapes, and Roscius for a tongue,   10
So could he speak, so vary; nor is't hate
To merit in ‡him who doth personate   ‡Perkins.
Our Jew this day, nor is it his ambition
To exceed, or equal, being of condition
More modest; this is all that he intends,   15
(And that too, at the urgence of some friends)
To prove his best, and if none here gainsay it,
The part he hath studied, and intends to play it.

EPILOGUE

In graving, with Pygmalion to contend;
Or painting, with Apelles; doubtless the end
Must be disgrace: our actor did not so,
He only aimed to go, but not out-go.
Nor think that this day any prize was played,   5
Here were no bets at all, no wagers laid;
All the ambition that his mind doth swell,
Is but to hear from you (by me) 'twas well.

Prologue
    7 *wan* won
    10 *Proteus* a sea-god who could 'vary' his shape at will
       Roscius a Roman actor
    12 *Perkins* Richard Perkins, acting *c.* 1602–1635
    14 *condition* character
Epilogue
    1 *graving* sculpture
    1, 2 *Pygmalion, Apelles* Greek sculptor and painter of legendary skill
    5 *prize was played* special show of skill was made (metaphor from an
    exhibition fencing-match)

DRAMATIS PERSONAE

MACHEVILL, the Prologue
BARABAS, the Jew *DIES*
GOVERNOR of Malta (FERNEZE)
SELIM-CALYMATH, the Turkish leader, son to the Grand Seigneur *D*
DIE MATHIAS, a young gentleman } both in love with Abigail
LODOWICK, the Governor's son
MARTIN DEL BOSCO, the Spanish Vice-Admiral
DIE ITHAMORE, a Turkish slave
PILIA-BORZA, a Courtesan's bully
DIE Two FRIARS { 1 JACOMO
2 BARNARDINE
Two MERCHANTS; three JEWS; KNIGHTS; BASSOES; OFFICERS;
GUARD; SLAVES; MESSENGER; CARPENTERS
DIES ABIGAIL, daughter to Barabas
MOTHER of Mathias (KATHERINE)
DIE COURTESAN (BELLAMIRA)
ABBESS
NUN

No list of *Dramatis Personae* is supplied by Q

7

THE JEW OF MALTA

[THE PROLOGUE]

MACHEVILL

Albeit the world think Machevill is dead,
Yet was his soul but flown beyond the Alps,
And now the Guise is dead, is come from France
To view this land, and frolic with his friends.
To some perhaps my name is odious,   5
But such as love me, guard me from their tongues,
And let them know that I am Machevill,
And weigh not men, and therefore not men's words.
Admired I am of those that hate me most.
Though some speak openly against my books,   10
Yet will they read me, and thereby attain
To Peter's chair: and when they cast me off,
Are poisoned by my climbing followers.
I count religion but a childish toy,
And hold there is no sin but ignorance.   15
Birds of the air will tell of murders past?
I am ashamed to hear such fooleries.
Many will talk of title to a crown.
What right had Caesar to the empery?
Might first made kings, and laws were then most sure   20

---

4 *this land* England *cf.* line 29   6 *guard* protect
8 *weigh* value   12 *Peter's chair* the Papacy
16 *past?* ed. (Q past;)   19 *empery* ed. (Q Empire)

---

1 *Machevill*: Machiavelli (for the English pronunciation *cf.* Heywood's
Prologue spoken at Court, 8), here typifying the villainous self-interested
calculation for which he was a by-word in Elizabethan times. This
prologue-soliloquy is based upon a Latin epigram of 26 lines by Gabriel
Harvey (1578), headed *Machiavellus ipse loquitur* ('Machiavelli himself
speaks'); this is given in translation by Poirier, pp. 48–9.

3 *the Guise*: Duke of Guise, French statesman, responsible for the St
Bartholomew massacre of Protestants in 1572, and hence hated by
English Protestants. Assassinated 23rd December 1588. See Marlowe's
play *The Massacre at Paris*.

9

When like the Draco's they were writ in blood.
Hence comes it, that a strong built citadel
Commands much more than letters can import:
Which maxim had but Phalaris observed,
H'had never bellowed in a brazen bull   25
Of great ones' envy; o' th' poor petty wits,
Let me be envied and not pitièd!
But whither am I bound, I come not, I,
To read a lecture here in Britanie,
But to present the tragedy of a Jew,   30
Who smiles to see how full his bags are crammed,
Which money was not got without my means.
I crave but this, grace him as he deserves,
And let him not be entertained the worse
Because he favours me.   35

                                              [*Exit*]

21 *Draco's* ed. (Q *Drancus*)
24 *had but Phalaris* ed. (Q had *Phaleris*)
26 *wits* ed. (Q *wites*)
29 *Britanie* ed. (Q *Britaine*)
35 *favours* resembles

---

21 *Draco*: author of sharp Athenian laws, *c.* 624 B.C.; 'writ in blood' is a
  contemporary's comment on them.
24 *Phalaris*: Sicilian tyrant, *c.* 570–554 B.C. He roasted his enemies alive
  in an oven shaped like a bull, in which he himself perished at last, after
  a revolution which Machiavelli here says he should have been prepared
  to suppress, instead of writing letters (alluding to the *Letters of Phalaris*,
  supposed genuine in Marlowe's time, but really written much later
  than Phalaris lived). Machiavelli's point is that strength is more important than culture.
33–5 An ingenious device: Machiavelli's recommendation is as good as
  dispraise.

[Act I, Scene i]

Enter BARABAS *in his counting-house,*
with heaps of gold before him

VOLPONE

BARABAS

So that of thus much that return was made:
And of the third part of the Persian ships,
There was the venture summed and satisfied.
As for those Samnites, and the men of Uz,
That bought my Spanish oils, and wines of Greece,   5
Here have I pursed their paltry silverlings.
Fie; what a trouble 'tis to count this trash!
Well fare the Arabians, who so richly pay
The things they traffic for with wedge of gold,   *- GOOD IMAGE OF GOLD PIE.*
Whereof a man may easily in a day   10
Tell that which may maintain him all his life.
The needy groom that never fingered groat,
Would make a miracle of thus much coin:
But he whose steel-barred coffers are crammed full,
And all his life-time hath been tirèd,   15
Wearying his fingers' ends with telling it,
Would in his age he loath to labour so,
And for a pound to sweat himself to death:
Give me the merchants of the Indian mines,
That trade in metal of the purest mould;   20
The wealthy Moor, that in the Eastern rocks

1 speaker's name *Barabas* ed. (Q *Iew*, throughout scene)
4 *Samnites* ed. (Q *Samintes*)
6 *silverlings* silver coins
9 *traffic for* barguin for
11 *Tell* count
12 *groom* servant, slave (derogatory)

---

1 'Is there another English play before *The Jew of Malta* which opens in mid-speech?' (Wilson). This opening dramatically presents Barabas's absorption with his wealth. He 'enters' by being discovered, as the curtains of the inner-stage are parted.
4 *Samnites*: Inhabitants of part of Southern Italy. Various emendations have been proposed, none wholly convincing. It is likely that 'Samnites' and 'men of Uz' (Job i.1) are both used casually by Marlowe to suggest the Mediterranean and Middle East: *cf.* Kirriah Jairim (I.i, 126), really the name of a city (Joshua xv. 9; Judges xviii. 12), but given by Marlowe to an imaginary person.

Without control can pick his riches up,
And in his house heap pearl like pibble-stones,
Receive them free, and sell them by the weight;
Bags of fiery opals, sapphires, amethysts,   25
Jacinths, hard topaz, grass-green emeralds,
Beauteous rubies, sparkling diamonds,
And seld-seen costly stones of so great price,
As one of them indifferently rated,
And of a caract of this quantity,   30
May serve in peril of calamity
To ransom great kings from captivity.
This is the ware wherein consists my wealth:
And thus methinks should men of judgement frame
Their means of traffic from the vulgar trade,   35
And as their wealth increaseth, so inclose
Infinite riches in a little room.
But now how stands the wind?
Into what corner peers my halcyon's bill?
Ha, to the East? Yes. See how stands the vanes?   40
East and by South: why then I hope my ships
I sent for Egypt and the bordering isles
Are gotten up by Nilus' winding banks:
Mine argosy from Alexandria,
Loaden with spice and silks, now under sail,   45
Are smoothly gliding down by Candy shore
To Malta, through our Mediterranean sea.
But who comes here? How now.

Enter a MERCHANT

28 *seld-seen* ed. (Q seildsene) seldom seen, rare
29 *indifferently rated* fairly valued
30 *caract* ed. (Q Carrect) carat, measure of weight
34–35 *frame . . . vulgar trade* i.e. contrive not to use common coin
    in their trading
37 *room* space
44 *argosy* large merchant ship
46 *Candy* Crete

---

37 *Infinite riches in a little room.* Hunter detects in this line a materialistic
    application of an idea very common in devotional literature both before
    and after Marlowe, that of Christ's infinite power and value being
    enclosed within the womb of a humble virgin; thus the greedy un-
    believer's treasure is contrasted with the spiritual treasure embodied in
    Christ.
39 *halcyon*: a dead kingfisher was popularly supposed to turn according to
    the wind's direction.

MERCHANT
    Barabas, thy ships are safe,
    Riding in Malta road: and all the merchants   50
    With all their merchandise are safe arrived,
    And have sent me to know whether yourself
    Will come and custom them.
BARABAS
    The ships are safe thou say'st, and richly fraught?
MERCHANT
    They are.   55
BARABAS
    Why then go bid them come ashore,
    And bring with them their bills of entry:
    I hope our credit in the custom-house
    Will serve as well as I were present there.
    Go send 'em threescore camels, thirty mules,   60
    And twenty waggons to bring up the ware.
    But art thou master in a ship of mine,
    And is thy credit not enough for that?
MERCHANT
    The very custom barely comes to more
    Than many merchants of the town are worth,   65
    And therefore far exceeds my credit, sir.
BARABAS
    Go tell 'em the Jew of Malta sent thee, man:
    Tush, who amongst 'em knows not Barabas?
MERCHANT
    I go.
BARABAS
    So then, there's somewhat come.   70
    Sirrah, which of my ships art thou master of?
MERCHANT
    Of the Speranza, sir.
BARABAS
    And saw'st thou not
    Mine argosy at Alexandria?
    Thou couldst not come from Egypt, or by Caire,   75

---

50 *road* ed. (Q Rhode [frequently]) harbour
51 *all their* ed. (Q other)
53 *custom them* see them through the customs

70–1 'The first five words of Barabas are to himself. Then he shouts at
    the departing merchant, and, by an effective touch, inquires which of
    his numerous ships he commands' (Bennett).

But at the entry there into the sea,
Where Nilus pays his tribute to the main,
Thou needs must sail by Alexandria.

MERCHANT

I neither saw them, nor inquired of them.
But this we heard some of our seamen say,   80
They wondered how you durst with so much wealth
Trust such a crazèd vessel, and so far.

BARABAS

Tush; they are wise, I know her and her strength:
But go, go thou thy ways, discharge thy ship,
And bid my factor bring his loading in.   85

                          [*Exit* MERCHANT]

And yet I wonder at this argosy.

Enter a SECOND MERCHANT

2 MERCHANT

Thine argosy from Alexandria,
Know Barabas doth ride in Malta road,
Laden with riches, and exceeding store
Of Persian silks, of gold, and orient pearl.   90

BARABAS

How chance you came not with those other ships
That sailed by Egypt?

2 MERCHANT

Sir we saw 'em not.

BARABAS

Belike they coasted round by Candy shore
About their oils, or other businesses.   95
But 'twas ill done of you to come so far
Without the aid or conduct of their ships.

2 MERCHANT

Sir, we were wafted by a Spanish fleet
That never left us till within a league,
That had the galleys of the Turk in chase.   100

BARABAS

Oh they were going up to Sicily: well, go
And bid the merchants and my men dispatch
And come ashore, and see the fraught discharged.

82 *crazèd* frail
84 *But* ed. (Q By)
85 *factor* agent
91 *How chance* how happens it
100 *had ... in chase* were pursuing, *cf.* II.ii, 12

2 MERCHANT
  I go.

                                                              Exit

BARABAS
  Thus trowls our fortune in by land and sea,   105
  And thus are we on every side enriched:
  These are the blessings promised to the Jews,
  And herein was old Abram's happiness:
  What more may heaven do for earthly man
  Than thus to pour out plenty in their laps,   110
  Ripping the bowels of the earth for them,
  Making the sea their servant, and the winds
  To drive their substance with successful blasts?
  Who hateth me but for my happiness?
  Or who is honoured now but for his wealth?   115
  Rather had I a Jew be hated thus,
  Than pitied in a Christian poverty:
  For I can see no fruits in all their faith,
  But malice, falsehood, and excessive pride,
  Which methinks fits not their profession.   120
  Haply some hapless man hath conscience,
  And for his conscience lives in beggary.
  They say we are a scattered nation:
  I cannot tell, but we have scambled up
  More wealth by far than those that brag of faith.   125
  There's Kirriah Jairim, the great Jew of Greece,
  Obed in Bairseth, Nones in Portugal,
  Myself in Malta, some in Italy,
  Many in France, and wealthy every one:
  Ay, wealthier far than any Christian.   130
  I must confess we come not to be kings:
  That's not our fault: alas, our number's few,
  And crowns come either by succession
  Or urged by force; and nothing violent,

---

105 *trowls* rolls
108 *Abram* Abraham
112 *servant* ed. (Q seruants)
120 *their profession* their declared faith, alleged principles
124 *scambled up* raked together

107–8 'Luther, in his extended commentary on Galatians (published in
      English in 1575), notes how the Jews use Abraham's blessing "applying
      it only to a carnal blessing, and do great injury to Scripture".' (Hunter,
      alluding to Galatians iii. 13–16, 29.)
121–2 Those few Christians who do live honestly are poor for their pains:
      their fellows do nothing for them.

Oft have I heard tell, can be permanent.   135
Give us a peaceful rule, make Christians kings,
That thirst so much for principality.
I have no charge, nor many children,
But one sole daughter, whom I hold as dear
As Agamemnon did his Iphigen: 140
And all I have is hers. But who comes here?

Enter THREE JEWS

1 JEW
Tush, tell not me, 'twas done of policy.
2 JEW.
Come therefore let us go to Barabas;
For he can counsel best in these affairs;
And here he comes.   145
BARABAS
Why how now countrymen?
Why flock you thus to me in multitudes?
What accident's betided to the Jews?
1 JEW
A fleet of warlike galleys, Barabas,
Are come from Turkey, and lie in our road: 150
And they this day sit in the council-house
To entertain them and their embassy.
BARABAS
Why let 'em come, so they come not to war;
Or let 'em war, so we be conquerors:
(*aside*) Nay, let 'em combat, conquer, and kill all,   155
So they spare me, my daughter, and my wealth.
1 JEW
Were it for confirmation of a league,
They would not come in warlike manner thus.
2 JEW
I fear their coming will afflict us all.
BARABAS
Fond men, what dream you of their multitudes?   160

---

137 *principality* power, rule   138 *charge* responsibility
139 *But* only   142 *of policy* through cunning
151 *they* i.e. our rulers   157 *Were it for* if it were merely for

---

140 Agamemnon was commanded to sacrifice his daughter Iphigenia to
Diana, in order to obtain a favourable wind for sailing to Troy.
147 *in multitudes*: Not ironical. The three Jews, here as in I.ii, represent 'all
the Jews in Malta'.

What need they treat of peace that are in league?
The Turks and those of Malta are in league.
Tut, tut, there is some other matter in't.
1 JEW
Why, Barabas, they come for peace or war.
BARABAS
Haply for neither, but to pass along   165
Towards Venice by the Adriatic Sea;
With whom they have attempted many times,
But never could effect their stratagem.
3 JEW
And very wisely said, it may be so.
2 JEW
But there's a meeting in the senate-house,   170
And all the Jews in Malta must be there.
BARABAS
Umh; all the Jews in Malta must be there?
Ay, like enough, why then let every man
Provide him, and be there for fashion-sake.
If any thing shall there concern our state   175
Assure yourselves I'll look unto (*aside*) myself.
1 JEW
I know you will; well brethren let us go.
2 JEW
Let's take our leaves; farewell good Barabas.
BARABAS
Do so; farewell Zaareth, farewell Temainte.
                        [Exeunt the JEWS]
And Barabas now search this secret out.   180
Summon thy senses, call thy wits together:
These silly men mistake the matter clean.
Long to the Turk did Malta contribute;
Which tribute all in policy, I fear,
The Turks have let increase to such a sum   185
As all the wealth of Malta cannot pay;
And now by that advantage thinks, belike,
To seize upon the town: ay, that he seeks:

---

167 *With whom they have attempted* against whom (i.e. Venice) they
    have attempted [an attack]
172 *Umh* a reflective noise
174 *Provide him* prepare himself
174 *for fashion-sake* for the sake of appearances, as a matter of form
182 *clean* completely

---

176 Barabas leaves the Jews to assume that he ends his sentence with 'look
    unto our good', or some such phrase.

Howe'er the world go, I'll make sure for one,
And seek in time to intercept the worst,   190
Warily guarding that which I ha' got.
Ego mihimet sum semper proximus.
Why let 'em enter, let 'em take the town.

[*Exit*]

[Act I, Scene ii]

Enter GOVERNOR *of Malta*, KNIGHTS, [*and* OFFICERS,] *met
by* BASSOES *of the Turk*; [*and*] CALYMATH

GOVERNOR
Now bassoes, what demand you at our hands?
BASSO
Know knights of Malta, that we came from Rhodes,
From Cyprus, Candy, and those other isles
That lie betwixt the Mediterranean seas—
GOVERNOR
What's Cyprus, Candy, and those other isles   5
To us, or Malta? What at our hands demand ye?
CALYMATH
The ten years' tribute that remains unpaid.
GOVERNOR
Alas, my lord, the sum is over-great;
I hope your highness will consider us.
CALYMATH
I wish, grave Governor, 'twere in my power   10
To favour you, but 'tis my father's cause,
Wherein I may not, nay I dare not dally.
GOVERNOR
Then give us leave, great Selim-Calymath.
CALYMATH
Stand all aside, and let the knights determine,
And send to keep our galleys under sail,   15
For happily we shall not tarry here:
Now Governor, how are you resolved?
GOVERNOR
Thus: since your hard conditions are such

I.ii. s.d., 10, 17, 27, 33, 131 *Governor* ed. (Q Gouernors)
4 *seas*— ed. (Q seas.)   10 *grave* worthy
13 *give us leave* excuse ûs [while we consult]

192 A phrase from Terence's *Andria* (IV.i, 12), '*Proximus sum egomet mihi*',
adapted to blank verse. It might be paraphrased, 'I am my own dearest
friend'.

That you will needs have ten years' tribute past,
We may have time to make collection   20
Amongst the inhabitants of Malta for't.
BASSO
That's more than is in our commission.
CALYMATH
What Callapine, a little courtesy!
Let's know their time, perhaps it is not long;
And 'tis more kingly to obtain by peace   25
Than to enforce conditions by constraint.
What respite ask you Governor?
GOVERNOR
But a month.
CALYMATH
We grant a month, but see you keep your promise.
Now launch our galleys back again to sea,   30
Where we'll attend the respite you have ta'en,
And for the money send our messenger.
Farewell great Governor, and brave knights of Malta.
                    Exeunt [CALYMATH *and* BASSOES]
GOVERNOR
And all good fortune wait on Calymath.
Go one and call those Jews of Malta hither: 35
Were they not summoned to appear today?
OFFICER
They were, my lord, and here they come.
                    Enter BARABAS *and* THREE JEWS
1 KNIGHT
Have you determined what to say to them?
GOVERNOR
Yes, give me leave, and Hebrews now come near.
From the Emperor of Turkey is arrived   40
Great Selim-Calymath, his highness' son,
To levy of us ten years' tribute past;
Now then here know that it concerneth us—

22 *than is in our commission* than we are authorized to do
43 *concerneth us*— ed. (Q concerneth vs:)

---

43 *concerneth us*—. The interruption is characteristic of Barabas's be-
    haviour here. He is baiting the Governor, blandly advising him to pay
    up, and wilfully misunderstanding his phrase 'request your aid'. This
    helps to raise the tension before the crisis, Barabas's sneering 'How,
    equally?' (implying that they should pay less), and the Governor's
    retort 'No, Jew, like infidels' (implying that they shall pay more). A
    trap is certainly sprung upon Barabas; but if anyone deserves it, Barabas
    is the man.

BARABAS
Then good my lord, to keep your quiet still,
Your lordship shall do well to let them have it.   45
GOVERNOR
Soft Barabas, there's more 'longs to't than so.
To what this ten years' tribute will amount,
That we have cast, but cannot compass it
By reason of the wars, that robbed our store;
And therefore are we to request your aid.   50
BARABAS
Alas, my lord, we are no soldiers:
And what's our aid against so great a prince?
1 KNIGHT
Tut, Jew, we know thou art no soldier;
Thou art a merchant, and a moneyed man,
And 'tis thy money, Barabas, we seek.   55
BARABAS
How, my lord, my money?
GOVERNOR
Thine and the rest.
For to be short, amongst you 't must be had.
1 JEW
Alas, my lord, the most of us are poor!
GOVERNOR
Then let the rich increase your portions.   60
BARABAS
Are strangers with your tribute to be taxed?
2 KNIGHT
Have strangers leave with us to get their wealth?
Then let them with us contribute.
BARABAS
How, equally?
GOVERNOR
No, Jew, like infidels.   65
For through our sufferance of your hateful lives,
Who stand accursèd in the sight of heaven,
These taxes and afflictions are befallen,
And therefore thus we are determinèd:
Read there the articles of our decrees.   70

---

48 *cast* reckoned, calculated
   compass obtain, raise
58 *1 Jew* ed. (Q *Iew*)
60 *portions* shares of the contribution
67 *accursèd*, i.e. on account of the Crucifixion (*cf.* Matthew xxvii. 25)

OFFICER [*reads*]
First, the tribute money of the Turks shall all be levied
amongst the Jews, and each of them to pay one half of his
estate.

BARABAS
How, half his estate? I hope you mean not mine.

GOVERNOR
Read on.   75

OFFICER [*reads*]
Secondly, he that denies to pay, shall straight become a
Christian.

BARABAS
How, a Christian? Hum, what's here to do?

OFFICER [*reads*]
Lastly, he that denies this, shall absolutely lose all he has.

ALL 3 JEWS
Oh my lord we will give half.   80

BARABAS
Oh earth-metalled villains, and no Hebrews born!
And will you basely thus submit yourselves
To leave your goods to their arbitrement?

GOVERNOR
Why Barabas wilt thou be christenèd?

BARABAS
No, Governor, I will be no convertite.   85

GOVERNOR
Then pay thy half.

BARABAS
Why know you what you did by this device?
Half of my substance is a city's wealth.
Governor, it was not got so easily;
Nor will I part so slightly therewithal.   90

GOVERNOR
Sir, half is the penalty of our decree,

71, 76, 79 *Officer* [*reads*] ed. (Q *Reader*)
73 *estate* wealth
76 *denies* refuses
78 *what's here to do?* here's a business!
81 *earth-metalled* base-minded
83 *arbitrement* disposal
85 *convertite* convert
90 *slightly* easily, weakly

87 *did:* This use of the past tense is curious, where one would expect the
present. Perhaps 'doe' (do) was misread. An allusion to Christ's 'They
know not what they do' (Luke xxiii. 34) is not impossible: *cf.* next note.

Either pay that, or we will seize on all.
> [*Exeunt* OFFICERS, *on a sign from the* GOVERNOR]

BARABAS
Corpi di Dio; stay, you shall have half,
Let me be used but as my brethren are.

GOVERNOR
No, Jew, thou hast denied the articles,   95
And now it cannot be recalled.

BARABAS
Will you then steal my goods?
Is theft the ground of your religion?

GOVERNOR
No, Jew, we take particularly thine
To save the ruin of a multitude: 100
And better one want for a common good,
Than many perish for a private man:
Yet Barabas we will not banish thee,
But here in Malta, where thou got'st thy wealth,
Live still; and if thou canst, get more. — *TONE OF LINE?* 105

BARABAS
Christians; what, or how can I multiply?
Of nought is nothing made. *WHERE HEARD? KL!*

1 KNIGHT
From nought at first thou cam'st to little wealth,
From little unto more, from more to most:
If your first curse fall heavy on thy head,   110
And make thee poor and scorned of all the world,
'Tis not our fault, but thy inherent sin.

BARABAS
What? Bring you scripture to confirm your wrongs?
Preach me not out of my possessions.
Some Jews are wicked, as all Christians are: *STAGE WICKED-* 115
But say the tribe that I descended of   *NESS.*
Were all in general cast away for sin,
Shall I be tried by their transgression?
The man that dealeth righteously shall live:
And which of you can charge me otherwise?   120

---

93 *Corpo di Dio* (Italian) God's body
110 *your first curse*, i.e. that of the Jews, *cf.* line 67

101–2 'The plea of Caiaphas' (Boas): *cf.* John xi. 50. Hunter similarly sees
    an allusion to Pilate's washing his hands (Matthew xxvii. 24) in the
    Governor's lines 147–8.

GOVERNOR
    Out wretched Barabas,
    Sham'st thou not thus to justify thyself,
    As if we knew not thy profession?
    If thou rely upon thy righteousness,
    Be patient and thy riches will increase.   125
    Excess of wealth is cause of covetousness:
    And covetousness, oh 'tis a monstrous sin.

BURLESQUE

BARABAS
    Ay, but theft is worse: tush, take not from me then,
    For that is theft; and if you rob me thus,
    I must be forced to steal and compass more.   130

2 SCHOOLBOYS

1 KNIGHT
    Grave Governor, list not to his exclaims:
    Convert his mansion to a nunnery,
    His house will harbour many holy nuns.

                    Enter OFFICERS

GOVERNOR
    It shall be so: now officers, have you done?
OFFICER
    Ay, my lord, we have seized upon the goods   135
    And wares of Barabas, which being valued
    Amount to more than all the wealth in Malta.
    And of the other we have seizèd half.
GOVERNOR
    Then we'll take order for the residue.
BARABAS
    Well then my lord, say, are you satisfied?   140
    You have my goods, my money, and my wealth,
    My ships, my store, and all that I enjoyed;
    And having all, you can request no more;
    Unless your unrelenting flinty hearts
    Suppress all pity in your stony breasts,   145
    And now shall move you to bereave my life.
GOVERNOR
    No, Barabas, to stain our hands with blood
    Is far from us and our profession.

121 *Out* fie, for shame
123 *profession* [evil] principles (i.e. covetousness)
138 *the other* the other Jews
139 *Governor.* ed. (Q omits)
148 *profession* [good] principles (i.e. Christianity)

139 The meaning of 'the residue' is not clear. It may mean 'the balance of
    the tribute-money', or (as Spencer suggests) 'the rest of the business'.

BARABAS
Why, I esteem the injury far less,
To take the lives of miserable men,   150
Than be the causers of their misery.
You have my wealth, the labour of my life,
The comfort of mine age, my children's hope,
And therefore ne'er distinguish of the wrong.

GOVERNOR
Content thee, Barabas, thou hast nought but right.   155

BARABAS
Your extreme right does me exceeding wrong:
But take it to you i' the devil's name.

GOVERNOR
Come, let us in, and gather of these goods
The money for this tribute of the Turk.

1 KNIGHT
'Tis necessary that be looked unto: 160
For if we break our day, we break the league,
And that will prove but simple policy.
                    Exeunt [all except BARABAS *and* JEWS]

BARABAS
Ay, policy? that's their profession,
And not simplicity, as they suggest.
The plagues of Egypt, and the curse of heaven,   165
Earth's barrenness, and all men's hatred
Inflict upon them, thou great *Primus Motor.*
And here upon my knees, striking the earth,
I ban their souls to everlasting pains
And extreme tortures of the fiery deep,   170
That thus have dealt with me in my distress.

1 JEW
Oh yet be patient, gentle Barabas.

154 *distinguish of the wrong* make [false] distinctions between the
    wrongs (murder and theft)
155 *right* justice
157 *i' the* ed. (Q i' th')
162 *simple policy* foolish management
163 *policy* guile
167 *Primus Motor* (Latin) First Mover, i.e. God
169 *ban* curse

163–4 *Ay, policy?* An ironical repetition of the last speaker's last word.
    Barabas takes up the phrase 'simple policy' (foolish management), and
    interprets 'policy' as guile, in contrast to 'simplicity' or plain-dealing.

BARABAS
Oh silly brethren, born to see this day!
Why stand you thus unmoved with my laments?
Why weep you not to think upon my wrongs?   175
Why pine not I, and die in this distress?
1 JEW
Why, Barabas, as hardly can we brook
The cruel handling of ourselves in this:
Thou seèst they have taken half our goods.
BARABAS
Why did you yield to their extortion?   180
You were a multitude, and I but one,
And of me only have they taken all.
1 JEW
Yet brother Barabas remember Job.
BARABAS
What tell you me of Job? I wot his wealth
Was written thus: he had seven thousand sheep,   185
Three thousand camels, and two hundred yoke
Of labouring oxen, and five hundred
She asses: but for every one of those,
Had they been valued at indifferent rate,
I had at home, and in mine argosy   190
And other ships that came from Egypt last,
As much as would have bought his beasts and him,
And yet have kept enough to live upon;
So that not he, but I may curse the day,
Thy fatal birth-day, forlorn Barabas;   195
And henceforth wish for an eternal night,
That clouds of darkness may enclose my flesh,
And hide these extreme sorrows from mine eyes:
For only I have toiled to inherit here
The months of vanity and loss of time,   200
And painful nights have been appointed me.

173 *silly* wretched
177 *brook* endure
201 *have been* which have been

174–6 The repeated pattern of these lines is a stylistic device learned from
      Kyd's *Spanish Tragedy*. For other examples, see III.iii, 42–6 and III.v,
      36–7.
184–8 From Job i. 3, where, however, 'five hundred yoke of oxen' are
      mentioned. Further allusions to the Book of Job are made in 194–5
      (Job iii. 1) and 200–1 (Job vii. 3). Barabas's response to misfortune – he
      passes from impatience to a self-confidence which shows equal egoism –
      is to be contrasted with Job's resignation and confidence in God.

2 JEW
    Good Barabas be patient.

BARABAS
    Ay, I pray leave me in my patience.
    You that were ne'er possessed of wealth, are pleased with
                                                 want.
    But give him liberty at least to mourn,   205
    That in a field amidst his enemies,
    Doth see his soldiers slain, himself disarmed,
    And knows no means of his recovery:
    Ay, let me sorrow for this sudden chance;
    'Tis in the trouble of my spirit I speak;   210
    Great injuries are not so soon forgot.

1 JEW
    Come, let us leave him in his ireful mood,
    Our words will but increase his ecstasy.

2 JEW
    On then: but trust me 'tis a misery
    To see a man in such affliction: 215
    Farewell Barabas.

                                Exeunt [JEWS]

BARABAS
    Ay, fare you well.
    See the simplicity of these base slaves,
    Who, for the villains have no wit themselves,
    Think me to be a senseless lump of clay   220
    That will with every water wash to dirt:
    No, Barabas is born to better chance,
    And framed of finer mould than common men,
    That measure nought but by the present time.
    A reaching thought will search his deepest wits,   225
    And cast with cunning for the time to come:
    For evils are apt to happen every day.
    But whither wends my beauteous Abigail?

Enter ABIGAIL *the Jew's daughter*

213 *ecstasy* passion
218 *simplicity* stupidity
219 *for* because
219 *villains* wretches, 'base slaves'
225 *A reaching thought* a far-reaching thinker
226 *cast with cunning* cunningly calculate

225–6 These lines are not about Barabas's intentions but about his pre-
    cautions (i.e. the concealment of the wealth under his floor-boards,
    248–51): such precautions as a prudent man will, he says, always take.

Oh what has made my lovely daughter sad?
What? woman, moan not for a little loss: 230
Thy father has enough in store for thee.

ABIGAIL

Not for my self, but aged Barabas:
Father, for thee lamenteth Abigail:
But I will learn to leave these fruitless tears,
And urged thereto with my afflictions,   235
With fierce exclaims run to the senate-house,
And in the senate reprehend them all,
And rent their hearts with tearing of my hair,
Till they reduce the wrongs done to my father.

BARABAS

No, Abigail, things past recovery   240
Are hardly cured with exclamations.
Be silent, daughter, sufferance breeds ease,
And time may yield us an occasion,
Which on the sudden cannot serve the turn.
Besides, my girl, think me not all so fond   245
As negligently to forgo so much
Without provision for thyself and me.
Ten thousand portagues, besides great pearls,
Rich costly jewels, and stones infinite,
Fearing the worst of this before it fell,   250
I closely hid.

ABIGAIL

Where father?

BARABAS

In my house my girl.

ABIGAIL

Then shall they ne'er be seen of Barabas:
For they have seized upon thy house and wares.   255

BARABAS

But they will give me leave once more, I trow,
To go into my house.

236 *exclaims* exclamations
238 *rent* rend
239 *reduce* revoke
243–4 *And time ... serve the turn* and time, which cannot at this
  moment serve our turn, may grant us an opportunity
245 *fond* foolish
248 *portagues* gold coins

---

232 *Not for my self.* Abigail 'is characterized by the first four words she
  speaks' (Levin).
249 I suspect that 'jewels' and 'stones' have been transposed in this line.

ABIGAIL

That may they not:
For there I left the Governor placing nuns,
Displacing me; and of thy house they mean   260
To make a nunnery, where none but their own sect
Must enter in; men generally barred.

BARABAS

My gold, my gold, and all my wealth is gone.
You partial heavens, have I deserved this plague?
What, will you thus oppose me, luckless stars,   265
To make me desperate in my poverty?
And knowing me impatient in distress,
Think me so mad as I will hang myself,
That I may vanish o'er the earth in air,
And leave no memory that e'er I was?   270
No, I will live; nor loathe I this my life:
And since you leave me in the ocean thus
To sink or swim, and put me to my shifts,
I'll rouse my senses, and awake myself.
Daughter, I have it: thou perceiv'st the plight   275
Wherein these Christians have oppressèd me:
Be ruled by me, for in extremity
We ought to make bar of no policy.

ABIGAIL

Father, whate'er it be to injure them
That have so manifestly wrongèd us,   280
What will not Abigail attempt?

BARABAS

Why so;
Then thus, thou told'st me they have turned my house
Into a nunnery, and some nuns are there.

ABIGAIL

I did.   285

BARABAS

Then Abigail, there must my girl
Intreat the abbess to be entertained.

260 *they* the nuns
261 *sect* sex
262 *generally* without exception
265 *luckless* bringing ill-luck, malignant
273 *put me to my shifts* force me to take emergency action
278 *make bar of no policy* stick at no subterfuge
282 *Why so* that's right; very well, then
287 *entertained* received, admitted

ABIGAIL
  How, as a nun?
BARABAS
  Ay, daughter, for religion
  Hides many mischiefs from suspicion.   290
ABIGAIL
  Ay, but father they will suspect me there.
BARABAS
  Let 'em suspect, but be thou so precise
  As they may think it done of holiness.
  Intreat 'em fair, and give them friendly speech,
  And seem to them as if thy sins were great,   295
  Till thou hast gotten to be entertained.
ABIGAIL
  Thus father shall I much dissemble.
BARABAS
  Tush,
  As good dissemble that thou never mean'st
  As first mean truth, and then dissemble it;   300
  A counterfeit profession
  Is better than unseen hypocrisy.
ABIGAIL
  Well father, say I be entertained,
  What then shall follow?
BARABAS
  This shall follow then;   305
  There have I hid close underneath the plank
  That runs along the upper chamber floor,
  The gold and jewels which I kept for thee.
  But here they come; be cunning Abigail.
ABIGAIL
  Then father go with me.   310
BARABAS
  No, Abigail, in this
  It is not necessary I be seen.
  For I will seem offended with thee for't.
  Be close, my girl, for this must fetch my gold.

     [*Enter* TWO FRIARS, ABBESS, *and* NUN]

292 *precise* scrupulous
301 *counterfeit profession* falsely-pretended belief
303 *say* suppose
314 *close* cunning
314 s.d. ed. (Q *Enter three Fryars and two Nuns.*)

1 FRIAR

    Sisters, we now are almost at the new-made nunnery.   315

ABBESS

    The better; for we love not to be seen:

    'Tis thirty winters long since some of us

    Did stray so far amongst the multitude.

1 FRIAR

    But, madam, this house

    And waters of this new-made nunnery   320

    Will much delight you.

ABBESS

    It may be so: but who comes here?

ABIGAIL

    Grave abbess, and yon happy virgin's guide,

    Pity the state of a distressèd maid.

ABBESS

    What art thou daughter?   325

ABIGAIL

    The hopeless daughter of a hapless Jew,

    The Jew of Malta, wretched Barabas;

    Sometimes the owner of a goodly house,

    Which they have now turned to a nunnery.

ABBESS

    Well, daughter, say, what is thy suit with us?   330

ABIGAIL

    Fearing the afflictions which my father feels

    Proceed from sin, or want of faith in us,

    I'd pass away my life in penitence,

    And be a novice in your nunnery,

    To make atonement for my labouring soul.   335

1 FRIAR

    No doubt, brother, but this proceedeth of the spirit.

---

316 *Abbess* ed. (Q *1 Nun*)
322 *Abbess* ed. (Q *Nun*)
323 *yon happy* ed. (Q you happy)
328 *Sometimes* sometime, formerly
334 *novice* probationer
335 *labouring* struggling [against evil]

---

323 Editors who follow the Q reading ('you') suppose that Abigail is address-
    ing first the Abbess and then the Friars; but if the emendation is
    accepted, the Abbess is addressed throughout, called the [spiritual]
    guide of the nun, and asked to guide Abigail also.
326 Imitated from Kyd's *Spanish Tragedy*, IV.iv. 84, 'The hopeless father
    of a hapless son' (Bradbrook).

2 FRIAR

    Ay, and of a moving spirit too, brother; but come,
    Let us intreat she may be entertained.

ABBESS

    Well, daughter, we admit you for a nun.

ABIGAIL

    First let me as a novice learn to frame   340
    My solitary life to your strait laws,
    And let me lodge where I was wont to lie;
    I do not doubt by your divine precepts
    And mine own industry, but to profit much.

BARABAS (*aside*)

    As much I hope as all I hid is worth.   345

ABBESS

    Come daughter, follow us.

BARABAS

    Why how now Abigail,
    What mak'st thou amongst these hateful Christians?

1 FRIAR

    Hinder her not, thou man of little faith,
    For she has mortified herself.   350

BARABAS

    How, mortified!

1 FRIAR

    And is admitted to the sisterhood.

BARABAS

    Child of perdition, and thy father's shame,
    What wilt thou do among these hateful fiends?
    I charge thee on my blessing that thou leave   355
    These devils, and their damnèd heresy.

ABIGAIL

    Father forgive me—

348 *What mak'st thou* what are you doing
350 *has mortified herself* has died to the world
357 *forgive* ed. (Q giue)

336–7 Submerged blank verse: 'No doubt [, brother,] but this proceedeth
of the spirit'. '[Ay,] and of a moving spirit too [, brother]; but come'.
Thus, while comic in their mannerism, the speeches harmonize with
the surrounding regular verse.

357 *Father, forgive me*—. Abigail runs to Barabas, and this covers his aside.
The line 'The board is marked thus that covers it' is repeated at line
366, in italics to show that it is an aside, and with an obelisk to show
where Barabas makes a descriptive sign. This italicized version may
perhaps be a corrected form of its first appearance, as it interrupts two
lines (365, 367) addressed to the Friar, and seems out of place (the other
asides in that speech are mixed with his audible address to Abigail).

BARABAS (*whispers to her*)
Nay back, Abigail,
And think upon the jewels and the gold,
The board is marked thus that covers it. —   360
Away accursed from thy father's sight.

1 FRIAR
Barabas, although thou art in misbelief,
And wilt not see thine own afflictions,
Yet let thy daughter be no longer blind.

BARABAS
Blind friar, I reck not thy persuasions   365
[*aside*] The board is marked thus † that covers it,
For I had rather die, than see her thus.
Wilt thou forsake me too in my distress,
Seducèd daughter, (*aside to her*) Go forget not.—
Becomes it Jews to be so credulous?   370
(*aside to her*) Tomorrow early I'll be at the door.—
No come not at me, if thou wilt be damned,
Forget me, see me not, and so be gone.
(*aside*) Farewell. Remember tomorrow morning.—
Out, out thou wretch.   375

    [*Exeunt: on the one side*, BARABAS; *on the other*, FRIARS,
    ABBESS, NUN, *and* ABIGAIL]

Enter MATHIAS

MATHIAS
Who's this? Fair Abigail the rich Jew's daughter
Become a nun! Her father's sudden fall
Has humbled her and brought her down to this:
Tut, she were fitter for a tale of love
Than to be tired out with orisons: 380
And better would she far become a bed
Embracèd in a friendly lover's arms,
Than rise at midnight to a solemn mass.

Enter LODOWICK

LODOWICK
Why how now Don Mathias, in a dump?

MATHIAS
Believe me, noble Lodowick, I have seen   385
The strangest sight, in my opinion,
That ever I beheld.

365 *Blind friar*, ed. (Q Blind, Fryer,)
365 *reck* ed. (Q wrecke) heed   380 *orisons* prayers
384 *in a dump* sunk in reflection or gloom

LODOWICK
  What was't, I prithee?
MATHIAS
  A fair young maid scarce fourteen years of age,
  The sweetest flower in Cytherea's field,   390
  Cropt from the pleasures of the fruitful earth,
  And strangely metamorphosed to a nun.
LODOWICK
  But say, what was she?
MATHIAS
  Why the rich Jew's daughter.
LODOWICK
  What Barabas, whose goods were lately seized?   395
  Is she so fair?
MATHIAS
  And matchless beautiful;
  As had you seen her 'twould have moved your heart,
  Though countermured with walls of brass, to love,
  Or at the least to pity.   400
LODOWICK
  And if she be so fair as you report,
  'Twere time well spent to go and visit her:
  How say you, shall we?
MATHIAS
  I must and will, sir, there's no remedy.
LODOWICK
  And so will I too, or it shall go hard.   405
  Farewell Mathias.
MATHIAS
  Farewell Lodowick.

                                                          Exeunt

Act II [Scene i]

Enter BARABAS *with a light*

BARABAS
  Thus like the sad presaging raven that tolls
  The sick man's passport in her hollow beak,
  And in the shadow of the silent night

390 *Cytherea* Venus
392 *metamorphosed to a nun* ed. (Q metamorphis'd Nun) transformed
    to a nun
399 *countermured* ed. (Q countermin'd) doubly walled for defence

Doth shake contagion from her sable wings,
Vexed and tormented runs poor Barabas   5
With fatal curses towards these Christians.
The incertain pleasures of swift-footed time
Have ta'en their flight, and left me in despair;
And of my former riches rests no more
But bare remembrance; like a soldier's scar,   10
That has no further comfort for his maim.
Oh thou that with a fiery pillar led'st
The sons of Israel through the dismal shades,
Light Abraham's offspring; and direct the hand
Of Abigail this night; or let the day   15
Turn to eternal darkness after this:
No sleep can fasten on my watchful eyes,
Nor quiet enter my distempered thoughts,
Till I have answer of my Abigail.

Enter ABIGAIL *above*

ABIGAIL
Now have I happily espied a time   20
To search the plank my father did appoint;
And here behold (unseen) where I have found
The gold, the pearls, and jewels which he hid.
BARABAS
Now I remember those old women's words,
Who in my wealth would tell me winter's tales,   25
And speak of spirits and ghosts that glide by night
About the place where treasure hath been hid:
And now methinks that I am one of those:
For whilst I live, here lives my soul's sole hope,
And when I die, here shall my spirit walk.   30
ABIGAIL
Now that my father's fortune were so good
As but to be about this happy place;
'Tis not so happy: yet when we parted last,
He said he would attend me in the morn.
Then, gentle sleep, wheree'er his body rests,   35
Give charge to Morpheus that he may dream
A golden dream, and of the sudden wake,
Come and receive the treasure I have found.

11 *maim* wound
25 *winter's tales* fanciful folk-stories
37 *wake* ed. (Q walke)

BARABAS
Bueno para todos mi ganado no era:
As good go on, as sit so sadly thus.　　　　　　　40
But stay, what star shines yonder in the East?
The loadstar of my life, if Abigail.
Who's there?

ABIGAIL
Who's that?

BARABAS
Peace, Abigail, 'tis I.　　　　　　　　　　　45

ABIGAIL
Then father here receive thy happiness.

(Throws down bags)

BARABAS
Hast thou't?

ABIGAIL
Here,
Hast thou't?
There's more, and more, and more.　　　　　　50

BARABAS
Oh my girl,
My gold, my fortune, my felicity;
Strength to my soul, death to mine enemy;
Welcome the first beginner of my bliss:
Oh Abigail, Abigail, that I had thee here too,　　　55
Then my desires were fully satisfied,
But I will practise thy enlargement thence:
Oh girl, oh gold, oh beauty, oh my bliss!

(Hugs his bags)

ABIGAIL
Father, it draweth towards midnight now,
And 'bout this time the nuns begin to wake;　　　60
To shun suspicion, therefore, let us part.

BARABAS
Farewell my joy, and by my fingers take
A kiss from him that sends it from his soul.

[*Exit* ABIGAIL]

39 *Bueno para todos mi ganado no era:* ed. (Q *Birn para todos, my ganada no er*) (Spanish) My flock was not good for all
42 *loadstar* pole star, guiding light
57 *practise thy enlargement* contrive your release

39 The proverb is cryptic and dramatically unhelpful, though it serves, like II.i, 68 and Barabas's foreign oaths, to remind us that he is even in the world of Malta a foreigner. Spencer interprets 'My wealth does not avail me in every emergency'.

Now Phoebus ope the eye-lids of the day,
And for the raven wake the morning lark,   65
That I may hover with her in the air,
Singing o'er these, as she does o'er her young.
Hermoso placer de los dineros.

         [Exit]

[Act II, Scene ii]

Enter GOVERNOR, MARTIN DEL BOSCO, *the* KNIGHTS [*and*
OFFICERS]

GOVERNOR

Now Captain tell us whither thou art bound?
Whence is thy ship that anchors in our road?
And why thou cam'st ashore without our leave?

BOSCO

Governor of Malta, hither am I bound;
My ship, the Flying Dragon, is of Spain,   5
And so am I, Del Bosco is my name;
Vice-admiral unto the Catholic king.

1 KNIGHT

'Tis true, my lord, therefore intreat him well.

BOSCO

Our fraught is Grecians, Turks, and Afric Moors,
For late upon the coast of Corsica,   10
Because we vailed not to the Turkish fleet,
Their creeping galleys had us in the chase:
But suddenly the wind began to rise,
And then we luffed, and tacked, and fought at ease:
Some have we fired, and many have we sunk;   15
But one amongst the rest became our prize:
The captain's slain, the rest remains our slaves,
Of whom we would make sale in Malta here.

GOVERNOR

Martin del Bosco, I have heard of thee;
Welcome to Malta, and to all of us;   20
But to admit a sale of these thy Turks

---

65 *for* instead of
68 *Hermoso placer de los dineros* ed. (Q *Hermoso Piarer, de les Denirch*)
(Spanish) beautiful pleasure of money
68 s.d. *Exit* ed. (Q *Exeunt*)
11 *vailed* lowered topsails or flags in respect
Turkish ed. (Q *Spanish*)
14 *luffed, and tacked* ed. (Q left, and tooke) turned into the wind and
changed course

We may not, nay we dare not give consent
By reason of a tributary league.

1 KNIGHT

Del Bosco, as thou lov'st and honour'st us,
Persuade our Governor against the Turk; 25
This truce we have is but in hope of gold,
And with that sum he craves might we wage war.

BOSCO

Will Knights of Malta be in league with Turks,
And buy it basely too for sums of gold?
My lord, remember that to Europe's shame, 30
The Christian isle of Rhodes, from whence you came,
Was lately lost, and you were stated here
To be at deadly enmity with Turks.

GOVERNOR

Captain we know it, but our force is small.

BOSCO

What is the sum that Calymath requires? 35

GOVERNOR

A hundred thousand crowns.

BOSCO

My lord and king hath title to this isle,
And he means quickly to expel you hence;
Therefore be ruled by me, and keep the gold:
I'll write unto his Majesty for aid, 40
And not depart until I see you free.

GOVERNOR

On this condition shall thy Turks be sold.
Go officers and set them straight in show.

[*Exeunt* OFFICERS]

Bosco, thou shalt be Malta's general;
We and our warlike knights will follow thee 45
Against these barbarous misbelieving Turks.

BOSCO

So shall you imitate those you succeed:
For when their hideous force invironed Rhodes,
Small though the number was that kept the town,

27 *he* the Turk
32 *stated* stationed
39 *ruled* advised

---

42 Marlowe thus contrives, first, the Governor's new attitude towards the
Turks, and, second, the introduction of Ithamore.

They fought it out, and not a man survived   50
To bring the hapless news to Christendom.
GOVERNOR
So will we fight it out; come, let's away:
Proud-daring Calymath, instead of gold,
We'll send thee bullets wrapt in smoke and fire:
Claim tribute where thou wilt, we are resolved,   55
Honour is bought with blood and not with gold.

Exeunt

[Act II, Scene iii]

Enter OFFICERS *with* SLAVES

1 OFFICER
This is the market-place, here let 'em stand:
Fear not their sale, for they'll be quickly bought.
2 OFFICER
Every one's price is written on his back,
And so much must they yield or not be sold.

[Enter BARABAS*]*

1 OFFICER
Here comes the Jew, had not his goods been seized,   5
He'd give us present money for them all.
BARABAS
In spite of these swine-eating Christians
(Unchosen nation, never circumcised;
Such as, poor villains, were ne'er thought upon
Till Titus and Vespasian conquered us),   10
Am I become as wealthy as I was:
They hoped my daughter would ha' been a nun;
But she's at home, and I have bought a house
As great and fair as is the Governor's;
And there in spite of Malta will I dwell: 15
Having Ferneze's hand, whose heart I'll have;

54 *send thee* ed. (Q send the)
    4 s.d. ed. (Q [marginally] *Ent. Bar.*; his speech beginning at line 7
    is then headed *Enter Barabas.*)
    6 *present money* cash

---

16 *Having Ferneze's hand.* This may mean that Barabas has a guarantee of
    safety written by the Governor, or perhaps that Barabas has the Gover-
    nor's formal friendship (pretending to shake hands and forget old
    injuries): the latter sense would make a better ironic contrast with
    Barabas's next words.

Ay, and his son's too, or it shall go hard.
I am not of the tribe of Levy, I,
That can so soon forget an injury.
We Jews can fawn like spaniels when we please;   20
And when we grin we bite, yet are our looks
As innocent and harmless as a lamb's.
I learned in Florence how to kiss my hand,
Heave up my shoulders when they call me dog,
And duck as low as any bare-foot friar,   25
Hoping to see them starve upon a stall,
Or else be gathered for in our synagogue;
That when the offering-basin comes to me,
Even for charity I may spit into't.
Here comes Don Lodowick the Governor's son,   30
One that I love for his good father's sake.

Enter LODOWICK

LODOWICK
I hear the wealthy Jew walkèd this way;
I'll seek him out, and so insinuate,
That I may have a sight of Abigail;
For Don Mathias tells me she is fair.   35
BARABAS [*aside*]
Now will I show myself to have more of the serpent than
the dove; that is, more knave than fool.
LODOWICK
Yond walks the Jew, now for fair Abigail.
BARABAS [*aside*]
Ay, ay, no doubt but she's at your command.
LODOWICK
Barabas, thou know'st I am the Governor's son.   40
BARABAS
I would you were his father too, sir, that's all the harm I
wish you: [*aside*] the slave looks like a hog's cheek new
singed.

---

25 *duck* bow humbly
27 *be gathered for* have a collection made for them
33 *insinuate* work myself into his favour

---

26 *starve upon a stall.* Not satisfactorily explained as 'exposed for sale, and
  starving for lack of purchasers' (Bennett), or starving in 'assigned
  quarters in an almshouse' (Spencer). It seems that a 'stall' here means
  an object on which beggars might sit or stand in full public view in
  order to ask alms; *cf.* next line.

LODOWICK
Whither walk'st thou Barabas?
BARABAS
No further: 'tis a custom held with us,   45
That when we speak with Gentiles like to you,
We turn into the air to purge ourselves:
For unto us the promise doth belong.
LODOWICK
Well, Barabas, canst help me to a diamond?
BARABAS
Oh, sir, your father had my diamonds.   50
Yet I have one left that will serve your turn:
(*aside*) I mean my daughter:—but ere he shall have her
I'll sacrifice her on a pile of wood.
I ha' the poison of the city for him,
And the white leprosy.   55
LODOWICK
What sparkle does it give without a foil?
BARABAS
The diamond that I talk of, ne'er was foiled:
[*aside*] But when he touches it, it will be foiled:—
Lord Lodowick, it sparkles bright and fair.
LODOWICK
Is it square or pointed, pray let me know.   60
BARABAS
Pointed it is, good sir,–(*aside*) but not for you.
LODOWICK
I like it much the better.
BARABAS
So do I too.

47 *purge* cleanse
56 *foil* metal leaf placed under a gem to increase its brilliance
57 *foiled* set by a jeweller
58 *foiled* defiled
61 *Pointed* [here means also] appointed

---

48 *the promise.* Hunter compares I.i, 107–8, observing that 'the "promise" was the very thing that the Gentiles were supposed to have been given', and quoting Romans iv. 13.

52 *Aside.* This is printed opposite line 53 in Q, probably because line 52 is too full of text for its inclusion. 'I mean my daughter' is said to the audience, not to Lodowick, for Lodowick and Barabas continue talking of Abigail obliquely as a diamond.

54 *The poison of the city.* Not satisfactorily explained either with reference to his Ancona poison of III.iv, 69 (Bennett) or as a corruption of the text. As it is associated with 'the white leprosy', I suppose it to be another natural disease which Barabas would willingly give to Lodowick, perhaps the plague, which might fairly be called 'the poison of the city'.

LODOWICK

How shows it by night?

BARABAS

Outshines Cynthia's rays:　　　　　　　　　　　　65
You'll like it better far a-nights than days.

LODOWICK

And what's the price?

BARABAS [*aside*]

Your life and if you have it.—O my lord
We will not jar about the price; come to my house
And I will giv't your honour (*aside*)–with a vengeance.　　　70

LODOWICK

No, Barabas, I will deserve it first.

BARABAS

Good sir,
Your father has deserved it at my hands,
Who of mere charity and Christian ruth,
To bring me to religious purity,　　　　　　　　　75
And as it were in catechizing sort,
To make me mindful of my mortal sins,
Against my will, and whether I would or no,
Seized all I had, and thrust me out-a-doors,
And made my house a place for nuns most chaste.　　　80

LODOWICK

No doubt your soul shall reap the fruit of it.

BARABAS

Ay, but my lord, the harvest is far off:
And yet I know the prayers of those nuns
And holy friars, having money for their pains,
Are wondrous: (*aside*) and indeed do no man good:—　　　85
And seeing they are not idle, but still doing,
'Tis likely they in time may reap some fruit,
I mean in fulness of perfection.

---

68 Q, marginally, *aside*; perhaps this s.d. belongs to Barabas's next
　　words
69 *jar* quarrel
74 *ruth* pity
76 *as it were in catechizing sort* like a spiritual instructor
86 *still doing* always active

---

66 This is surely Barabas's encouragement to Lodowick, drawing on his
　　eager question about the price. All the other remarks 'aside' are clear
　　statements of hatred and malice. There was no room for the word
　　'aside' in line 68.
85 *aside*. The whole phrase is printed in italics, but probably only the
　　words 'no man', which reverse the sense, are spoken aside.

LODOWICK
Good Barabas glance not at our holy nuns.

BARABAS
No, but I do it through a burning zeal,   90
(*aside*) Hoping ere long to set the house afire;
For though they do awhile increase and multiply,
I'll have a saying to that nunnery.—
As for the diamond, sir, I told you of,
Come home and there's no price shall make us part,   95
Even for your honourable father's sake.
(*aside*) It shall go hard but I will see your death.—
But now I must be gone to buy a slave.

LODOWICK
And, Barabas, I'll bear thee company.

BARABAS
Come then, here's the market-place; what's the price of   100
this slave, two hundred crowns? Do the Turks weigh so
much?

1 OFFICER
Sir, that's his price.

BARABAS
What, can he steal that you demand so much?
Belike he has some new trick for a purse;   105
And if he has, he is worth three hundred plats,
So that, being bought, the town-seal might be got
To keep him for his life time from the gallows.
The sessions day is critical to thieves,
And few or none scape but by being purged.   110

89 *glance at* cast aspersions upon
93 *have a saying to* have something to say to, deal with
101 *Turks* ed. (Q *Turke*)
105 *new trick for* new way of stealing
106 *And if* supposing
    plats pieces of money
107 *So that* if only

96–7 The aside makes this into a complete sentence announcing that
    Barabas will revenge himself on the Governor by killing Lodowick.
98 An abrupt change of subject. Barabas's conversation with Lodowick
    has been unlocalized, and he does not reach the market-place till two
    lines later; but when he entered near the scene's beginning, the Officers
    at the market-place pointed him out. The whole handling of place and
    time in this play is loose and free: the progress of the dramatic action
    is more important to Marlowe than such consistency.
109–10 There is medical imagery in 'critical' and 'purged': Barabas says
    that few thieves get through the dangerous sessions day (or assizes)
    without being 'purged' (euphemism for 'hanged').

LODOWICK
Ratest thou this Moor but at two hundred plats?
1 OFFICER
No more, my lord.
BARABAS
Why should this Turk be dearer than that Moor?
1 OFFICER
Because he is young and has more qualities.
BARABAS
What, hast the philosopher's stone? And thou hast, break   115
my head with it, I'll forgive thee.
SLAVE
No sir, I can cut and shave.
BARABAS
Let me see, sirrah, are you not an old shaver?
SLAVE
Alas, sir, I am a very youth.
BARABAS
A youth? I'll buy you, and marry you to Lady Vanity, if   120
you do well.
SLAVE
I will serve you, sir.
BARABAS
Some wicked trick or other. It may be under colour of
shaving, thou'lt cut my throat for my goods. Tell me, hast
thou thy health well?   125
SLAVE
Ay, passing well.
BARABAS
So much the worse; I must have one that's sickly, and 't be
but for sparing vittles: 'tis not a stone of beef a day will
maintain you in these chops; let me see one that's somewhat
leaner.   130
1 OFFICER
Here's a leaner, how like you him?

115 *philosopher's stone* supposed mineral capable of turning base
      metals into gold
117, 119, 122, 126 *Slave* ed. (Q *Itha.* or *Ith.*)
126 *passing well* excellently
127–8 *and 't be but for* ed. (Q And be but for) if only for the sake of
129 *in these chops* with such jowls

119–20 *Youth* and *Vanity* are both names of morality-play characters.
      Barabas is playfully perverse: of course, a Youth who 'did well' would
      forsake Vanity, and embrace Virtue or Good Counsel.

BARABAS
  Where wast thou born?
ITHAMORE
  In Thrace; brought up in Arabia.
BARABAS
  So much the better, thou art for my turn;
  An hundred crowns, I'll have him; there's the coin.   135
1 OFFICER
  Then mark him, sir, and take him hence.
BARABAS [*aside*]
  Ay, mark him, you were best, for this is he
  That by my help shall do much villainy.
  My lord farewell. Come sirrah you are mine.
  As for the diamond it shall be yours;   140
  I pray, sir, be no stranger at my house,
  All that I have shall be at your command.

Enter MATHIAS [*and his* MOTHER]

MATHIAS [*aside*]
  What makes the Jew and Lodowick so private?
  I fear me 'tis about fair Abigail.
BARABAS
  Yonder comes Don Mathias, let us stay;   145
  He loves my daughter, and she holds him dear:
  But I have sworn to frustrate both their hopes,
  And be revenged upon the — [*aside*] Governor.
                                         [*Exit* LODOWICK]
MOTHER
  This Moor is comeliest, is he not? speak, son.
MATHIAS
  No, this is the better, mother, view this well.   150
BARABAS
  Seem not to know me here before your mother,
  Lest she mistrust the match that is in hand:
  When you have brought her home, come to my house;
  Think of me as thy father; son farewell.

132 *wast* ed. (Q was)
134 *for my turn* fit for me to use
136 *mark* put your mark on
137 *mark* note, observe
142 s.d. ed. (Q *Enter Mathias, Mater*; her speeches so headed through-
     out)
145 *stay* cease talking
152 *mistrust* suspect

MATHIAS
But wherefore talked Don Lodowick with you?   155
BARABAS
Tush man, we talked of diamonds, not of Abigail.
MOTHER
Tell me, Mathias, is not that the Jew?
BARABAS
As for the comment on the Maccabees,
I have it, sir, and 'tis at your command.
MATHIAS
Yes, madam, and my talk with him was but   160
About the borrowing of a book or two.
MOTHER
Converse not with him, he is cast off from heaven.
Thou hast thy crowns, fellow, come let's away.
MATHIAS
Sirrah, Jew, remember the book.
BARABAS
Marry will I, sir.   165
                Exeunt [MATHIAS *and his* MOTHER, *with a* SLAVE]
1 OFFICER
Come, I have made a reasonable market, let's away.
                              [*Exeunt* OFFICERS *with* SLAVES]
BARABAS
Now let me know thy name, and therewithal
Thy birth, condition, and profession.
ITHAMORE
Faith, sir, my birth is but mean, my name's Ithamore, my
profession what you please.   170
BARABAS
Hast thou no trade? then listen to my words,
And I will teach thee that shall stick by thee:
First be thou void of these affections,
Compassion, love, vain hope, and heartless fear,
Be moved at nothing, see thou pity none,   175
But to thyself smile when the Christians moan.
ITHAMORE
Oh brave, master, I worship your nose for this.

158 *comment* commentary
160 *was but* ed. (Q was)
165 s.d. (Q places after line 163)
172 *teach thee* ed. (Q teach)
172 *that shall stick by thee* what you shall profitably remember
174 *heartless* lacking spirit
177 *Oh brave* very good

BARABAS

As for myself, I walk abroad a-nights,
And kill sick people groaning under walls:
Sometimes I go about and poison wells;　　　　180
And now and then, to cherish Christian thieves,
I am content to lose some of my crowns;
That I may, walking in my gallery,
See 'em go pinioned along by my door.
Being young I studied physic, and began　　　　185
To practise first upon the Italian;
There I enriched the priests with burials,
And always kept the sexton's arms in ure
With digging graves and ringing dead men's knells:
And after that was I an engineer,　　　　190
And in the wars 'twixt France and Germany,
Under pretence of helping Charles the Fifth,
Slew friend and enemy with my stratagems.
Then after that was I an usurer,
And with extorting, cozening, forfeiting,　　　　195
And tricks belonging unto brokery,
I filled the jails with bankrouts in a year,
And with young orphans planted hospitals,
And every moon made some or other mad,
And now and then one hang himself for grief,　　　　200
Pinning upon his breast a long great scroll
How I with interest tormented him.
But mark how I am blest for plaguing them,
I have as much coin as will buy the town.
But tell me now, how hast thou spent thy time?　　　　205

ITHAMORE

Faith, master,
In setting Christian villages on fire,
Chaining of eunuchs, binding galley-slaves.
One time I was an hostler in an inn,
And in the night time secretly would I steal　　　　210
To travellers' chambers, and there cut their throats:
Once at Jerusalem, where the pilgrims kneeled,
I strowèd powder on the marble stones,

183 *gallery* balcony
188 *in ure* in use, busy
194 *usurer* money-lender
195 *cozening* cheating
196 *brokery* the dishonest practice of a broker
197 *bankrouts* bankrupts
198 *hospitals* almshouses
209 *hostler* stableman

And therewithal their knees would rankle, so
That I have laughed a-good to see the cripples   215
Go limping home to Christendom on stilts.

BARABAS

Why this is something: make account of me
As of thy fellow; we are villains both:
Both circumcisèd, we hate Christians both:
Be true and secret, thou shalt want no gold.   220
But stand aside, here comes Don Lodowick.

Enter LODOWICK

LODOWICK

Oh Barabas well met;
Where is the diamond you told me of?

BARABAS

I have it for you, sir; please you walk in with me:
What, ho, Abigail; open the door I say.   225

Enter ABIGAIL

ABIGAIL

In good time, father, here are letters come
From Ormus, and the post stays here within.

BARABAS

Give me the letters; daughter, do you hear?
Entertain Lodowick the Governor's son
With all the courtesy you can afford;   230
Provided that you keep your maidenhead.
Use him as if he were a (*aside*) Philistine.
Dissemble, swear, protest, vow to love him,
He is not of the seed of Abraham.—
I am a little busy, sir, pray pardon me.   235
Abigail, bid him welcome for my sake.

ABIGAIL

For your sake and his own he's welcome hither.

214 *rankle* fester
215 *a-good* heartily
227 *Ormus* a city on the Persian Gulf
     post messenger
228 *letters; daughter* ed. (Q letters, daughter)

---

232 As at I.i, 176, II.iii 148, and IV.iii, 30, the aside is the last word of
the phrase. Lodowick will assume that Barabas says 'as if he were a
prince'. Lodowick is meant to hear lines 229–31 also, with the jocular bad
taste of line 231. Line 235 refers not to Barabas's past aside, but to
his proposed withdrawal from their company to attend to business.

BARABAS

Daughter, a word more; [*aside*] kiss him, speak him fair,
And like a cunning Jew so cast about,
That ye be both made sure ere you come out.   240

ABIGAIL [*aside*]

Oh father, Don Mathias is my love.

BARABAS [*aside*]

I know it: yet I say make love to him;
Do, it is requisite it should be so.—
Nay on my life it is my factor's hand,
But go you in, I'll think upon the account: 245

[*Exeunt* ABIGAIL *and* LODOWICK]

The account is made, for Lodowick dies.
My factor sends me word a merchant's fled
That owes me for a hundred tun of wine:
I weigh it thus much; I have wealth enough.
For now by this has he kissed Abigail;   250
And she vows love to him, and he to her.
As sure as heaven rained manna for the Jews,
So sure shall he and Don Mathias die:
His father was my chiefest enemy.

Enter MATHIAS

Whither goes Don Mathias? Stay a while.   255

MATHIAS

Whither but to my fair love Abigail?

BARABAS

Thou know'st, and heaven can witness it is true,
That I intend my daughter shall be thine.

MATHIAS

Ay, Barabas, or else thou wrong'st me much.

BARABAS

Oh heaven forbid I should have such a thought.   260
Pardon me though I weep; the Governor's son
Will, whether I will or no, have Abigail:
He sends her letters, bracelets, jewels, rings.

MATHIAS

Does she receive them?

240 *made sure* betrothed
249 *thus much* i.e. not at all [snapping his fingers]
254 *was my chiefest enemy* i.e. 'in the late proceedings' (Spencer)
254 s.d. follows 255 in Q

249 *I have wealth enough.* refers both backward (to the slight loss) and forward (to the anticipated revenge).

BARABAS

  She? No, Mathias, no, but sends them back,   265
  And when he comes, she locks herself up fast;
  Yet through the key-hole will he talk to her,
  While she runs to the window looking out
  When you should come and hale him from the door.

MATHIAS

  Oh treacherous Lodowick!   270

BARABAS

  Even now as I came home, he slipt me in,
  And I am sure he is with Abigail.

MATHIAS

  I'll rouse him thence.

BARABAS

  Not for all Malta, therefore sheathe your sword;
  If you love me, no quarrels in my house;   275
  But steal you in, and seem to see him not;
  I'll give him such a warning ere he goes
  As he shall have small hopes of Abigail.
  Away, for here they come.

Enter LODOWICK, ABIGAIL

MATHIAS

  What hand in hand, I cannot suffer this.   280

BARABAS

  Mathias, as thou lov'st me, not a word.

MATHIAS

  Well, let it pass, another time shall serve.

Exit

LODOWICK

  Barabas, is not that the widow's son?

BARABAS

  Ay, and take heed, for he hath sworn your death.

LODOWICK

  My death? What, is the base-born peasant mad?   285

BARABAS

  No, no, but happily he stands in fear
  Of that which you, I think, ne'er dream upon;
  My daughter here, a paltry silly girl—

271 *slipt me in* slipped in, hurried inside
273 *rouse* drive [as a hunted beast from his lair]
286 *happily* haply
287 *that*, i.e. Lodowick's marriage with Abigail
    upon; ed. (Q vpon,)
288 *girl*— ed. (Q girle.)

LODOWICK
Why, loves she Don Mathias?
BARABAS
Doth she not with her smiling answer you?   290
ABIGAIL [*aside*]
He has my heart, I smile against my will.
LODOWICK
Barabas, thou know'st I have loved thy daughter long.
BARABAS
And so has she done you, even from a child.
LODOWICK
And now I can no longer hold my mind.
BARABAS
Nor I the affection that I bear to you.   295
LODOWICK
This is thy diamond, tell me, shall I have it?
BARABAS
Win it and wear it, it is yet unsoiled.
Oh but I know your lordship would disdain
To marry with the daughter of a Jew:
And yet I'll give her many a golden cross   300
With Christian posies round about the ring.
LODOWICK
'Tis not thy wealth, but her that I esteem,
Yet crave I thy consent.
BARABAS
And mine you have, yet let me talk to her;
(*aside*) This offspring of Cain, this Jebusite   305
That never tasted of the passover,
Nor e'er shall see the land of Canaan,
Nor our Messias that is yet to come,
This gentle maggot Lodowick I mean,
Must be deluded: let him have thy hand,   310
But keep thy heart till Don Mathias comes.
ABIGAIL [*aside*]
What, shall I be betrothed to Lodowick?
BARABAS [*aside*]
It's no sin to deceive a Christian;

294 *hold my mind* conceal my feelings, intentions
297 *unsoiled* pure, virginal
300 *cross* coin (stamped with a cross)
301 *with Christian . . . ring* having Christian mottoes round the coin's
    circumference

---

309 *This gentle maggot* a multiple pun on 'gentle', as meaning 'gentleman'
    and 'maggot', and as sounding like 'gentile'.

For they themselves hold it a principle,
Faith is not to be held with heretics;   315
But all are heretics that are not Jews;
This follows well, and therefore daughter fear not.—
I have intreated her, and she will grant.

LODOWICK
Then gentle Abigail plight thy faith to me.

ABIGAIL
I cannot choose, seeing my father bids: 320
Nothing but death shall part my love and me.

LODOWICK
Now have I that for which my soul hath longed.

BARABAS (*aside*)
So have not I, but yet I hope I shall.

ABIGAIL [*aside*]
Oh wretched Abigail, what hast thou done?

LODOWICK
Why on the sudden is your colour changed?   325

ABIGAIL
I know not, but farewell, I must be gone.

BARABAS
Stay her, but let her not speak one word more.

LODOWICK
Mute o' the sudden; here's a sudden change.

BARABAS
Oh muse not at it, 'tis the Hebrews' guise,
That maidens new betrothed should weep a while: 330
Trouble her not, sweet Lodowick depart:
She is thy wife, and thou shalt be mine heir.

LODOWICK
Oh, is't the custom, then I am resolved;
But rather let the brightsome heavens be dim,
And Nature's beauty choke with stifling clouds,   335
Than my fair Abigail should frown on me.
There comes the villain, now I'll be revenged.

Enter MATHIAS

317 *This follows well* this is good logic
324 *thou* ed. (Q thee)
327 *Stay* support
329 *guise* custom
333 *resolved* answered, reassured

321 Abigail says this openly (meaning Mathias), with intentional dramatic
irony. Lodowick naturally interprets it as her promise to himself.

BARABAS
Be quiet Lodowick, it is enough
That I have made thee sure to Abigail.
LODOWICK
Well, let him go.   340
                                          Exit

BARABAS
Well, but for me, as you went in at doors
You had been stabbed, but not a word on't now;
Here must no speeches pass, nor swords be drawn.
MATHIAS
Suffer me, Barabas, but to follow him.
BARABAS
No; so shall I, if any hurt be done,   345
Be made an accessary of your deeds;
Revenge it on him when you meet him next.
MATHIAS
For this I'll have his heart.
BARABAS
Do so; lo here I give thee Abigail.
MATHIAS
What greater gift can poor Mathias have?   350
Shall Lodowick rob me of so fair a love?
My life is not so dear as Abigail.
BARABAS
My heart misgives me, that to cross your love,
He's with your mother, therefore after him.
MATHIAS
What, is he gone unto my mother?   355
BARABAS
Nay, if you will, stay till she comes herself.
MATHIAS
I cannot stay; for if my mother come,
She'll die with grief.
                                          Exit

ABIGAIL
I cannot take my leave of him for tears:
Father, why have you thus incensed them both?   360
BARABAS
What's that to thee?
ABIGAIL
I'll make 'em friends again.
BARABAS
You'll make 'em friends? Are there not Jews enow in Malta
338 *quiet* calm

But thou must dote upon a Christian?

ABIGAIL
I will have Don Mathias, he is my love.   365

BARABAS
Yes, you shall have him. Go put her in.

ITHAMORE
Ay, I'll put her in.

[Puts ABIGAIL *in]*

BARABAS
Now tell me, Ithamore, how lik'st thou this?

ITHAMORE
Faith master, I think by this
You purchase both their lives; is it not so?   370

BARABAS
True; and it shall be cunningly performed.

ITHAMORE
Oh, master, that I might have a hand in this.

BARABAS
Ay, so thou shalt, 'tis thou must do the deed:
Take this and bear it to Mathias straight,
And tell him that it comes from Lodowick.   375

ITHAMORE
'Tis poisoned, is it not?

BARABAS
No, no, and yet it might be done that way:
It is a challenge feigned from Lodowick.

ITHAMORE
Fear not, I'll so set his heart afire,
That he shall verily think it comes from him.   380

BARABAS
I cannot choose but like thy readiness:
Yet be not rash, but do it cunningly.

ITHAMORE
As I behave myself in this, employ me hereafter.

BARABAS
Away then.

Exit [ITHAMORE]

So, now will I go in to Lodowick,   385
And like a cunning spirit feign some lie,
Till I have set 'em both at enmity.

Exit

370 *purchase* get, have
386 *spirit* devil

Act III [Scene i]

Enter a COURTESAN

COURTESAN

Since this town was besieged, my gain grows cold:
The time has been, that but for one bare night
A hundred ducats have been freely given:
But now against my will I must be chaste.
And yet I know my beauty doth not fail.   5
From Venice merchants, and from Padua
Were wont to come rare-witted gentlemen,
Scholars I mean, learned and liberal;
And now, save Pilia-Borza, comes there none,
And he is very seldom from my house;   10
And here he comes.

Enter PILIA-BORZA

PILIA-BORZA

Hold thee, wench, there's something for thee to spend.
                              [*Shows a bag of silver*]
COURTESAN

'Tis silver, I disdain it.
PILIA-BORZA

Ay, but the Jew has gold,
And I will have it or it shall go hard.   15
COURTESAN

Tell me, how cam'st thou by this?
PILIA-BORZA

Faith, walking the back lanes through the gardens, I chanced
to cast mine eye up to the Jew's counting-house, where I saw
some bags of money, and in the night I clambered up with
my hooks, and as I was taking my choice, I heard a rumbling   20
in the house; so I took only this, and run my way: but here's
the Jew's man.

Enter ITHAMORE

1 *my gain grows cold* my business grows slack

1 The siege does not begin till the Governor defies the Turks, III.v.
Bennett conjectures that the Courtesan's speech originally followed
that scene, which is possible. It is also possible that Marlowe originally
intended what is now III.v. to open the third act, but moved it to its
present position in order to divide the poisoning of the porridge from
the death of the nuns.

COURTESAN
Hide the bag.
PILIA-BORZA
Look not towards him, let's away: zoons what a looking
thou keep'st, thou'lt betray's anon.   25
                    [*Exeunt* COURTESAN *and* PILIA-BORZA]
ITHAMORE
O the sweetest face that ever I beheld! I know she is a
courtesan by her attire: now would I give a hundred of the
Jew's crowns that I had such a concubine.
Well, I have delivered the challenge in such sort,
As meet they will, and fighting die; brave sport.   30
                                                        Exit

[Act III, Scene ii]

Enter MATHIAS

MATHIAS
This is the place, now Abigail shall see
Whether Mathias holds her dear or no.

Enter LODOWICK *reading*

LODOWICK
What, dares the villain write in such base terms?

24 *zoons* God's wounds
25 *anon* at once
27 *attire* i.e. a 'loose-bodied flowing gown' (Bennett)
   s.d., 3–5 ed. Q reads:
            Enter Lodow. reading.
Math. What, dares the villain write in such base terms?
Lod. I did it, and reuenge it if thou dar'st.

3–5 Bennett guesses that 'something has fallen out' of the text here, and
   the two consecutive speech-headings for Mathias in Q make this a
   virtual certainty. The speech 'What, dares the villain write in such base
   terms.' must be Lodowick's: it is the dramatic consequence of the
   direction 'Enter Lodow. reading', and brings Lodowick on stage to the
   waiting Mathias, whose lost speech draws his reply 'I did it'. This
   cannot refer to a challenge: Marlowe is inconsistent about the challenge
   (saying in III.iii that Ithamore carried it to both rivals, whereas at the
   end of II.iii Ithamore was to incense Mathias and Barabas Lodowick),
   but the one consistent fact is that the challenge was forged, and so 'I did
   it' cannot possibly mean 'I wrote it'. Mathias's speech must have taxed
   Lodowick with rivalry over Abigail. If he used the word 'villain', the
   printer might easily overlook the line, being confused by the 'villain'
   in Lodowick's speech. Alternatively, if the lines were at the foot of a
   page of copy, one may have been torn off; but the repeated speech-
   heading makes the first alternative the more likely.

MATHIAS
[Thou villain, durst thou court my Abigail?]
LODOWICK
I did it, and revenge it if thou dar'st.   5

Fight. Enter BARABAS *above*

BARABAS
Oh bravely fought, and yet they thrust not home.
Now Lodowick, now Mathias, so;
                         [Both fall]
So, now they have showed themselves to be tall fellows.
[VOICES] (*within*)
Part 'em, part 'em.
BARABAS
Ay, part 'em now they are dead. Farewell, farewell.   10
                                   Exit

Enter GOVERNOR [*and* MATHIAS'S MOTHER, *with*
CITIZENS]

GOVERNOR
What sight is this? my Lodowick slain!
These arms of mine shall be thy sepulchre.
MOTHER
Who is this? my son Mathias slain!
GOVERNOR
Oh Lodowick! had'st thou perished by the Turk,
Wretched Ferneze might have venged thy death.   15
MOTHER
Thy son slew mine, and I'll revenge his death.
GOVERNOR
Look, Katherine, look, thy son gave mine these wounds.
MOTHER
O leave to grieve me, I am grieved enough.
GOVERNOR
Oh that my sighs could turn to lively breath;
And these my tears to blood, that he might live.   20
MOTHER
Who made them enemies?

8 *tall fellows* brave fellows
10 s.d. ed. (Q *Enter Gouernor. Mater.*)
18 *leave* cease
19 *lively* living, life-giving

---

12 Dyce compares *3 Henry VI*, II.v, 115:
           These arms of mine shall be thy winding sheet;
           My heart, sweet boy, shall be thy sepulchre.

GOVERNOR
　I know not, and that grieves me most of all.
MOTHER
　My son loved thine.
GOVERNOR
　And so did Lodowick him.
MOTHER
　Lend me that weapon that did kill my son,　　　　25
　And it shall murder me.
GOVERNOR
　Nay madam stay, that weapon was my son's,
　And on that rather should Ferneze die.
MOTHER
　Hold, let's inquire the causers of their deaths,
　That we may venge their blood upon their heads.　　　30
GOVERNOR
　Then take them up, and let them be interred
　Within one sacred monument of stone;
　Upon which altar I will offer up
　My daily sacrifice of sighs and tears,
　And with my prayers pierce impartial heavens,　　　35
　Till they disclose the causers of our smarts,
　Which forced their hands divide united hearts:
　Come, Katherine, our losses equal are,
　Then of true grief let us take equal share.
　　　　　　　　　　　　　　　Exeunt [with the bodies]

[Act III, Scene iii]

Enter ITHAMORE

ITHAMORE
　Why, was there ever seen such villainy,
　So neatly plotted, and so well performed?
　Both held in hand, and flatly both beguiled.

Enter ABIGAIL

36 *they disclose the* ed. (Q they the)
38 *Katherine* ed. (Q *Katherina*)
3 *held in hand* persuaded, falsely encouraged

36 *disclose.* Collier's conjecture suits the alliterative style (disclose, causers; *cf*. prayers, pierce; hands, hearts). Dyce, followed by most editors, reads 'reveal'.

ABIGAIL
Why how now Ithamore, why laugh'st thou so?
ITHAMORE
Oh, mistress, ha ha ha!   5
ABIGAIL
Why what ail'st thou?
ITHAMORE
Oh my master!
ABIGAIL
Ha?
ITHAMORE
Oh mistress! I have the bravest, gravest, secret, subtle
bottle-nosed knave to my master, that ever gentleman had!   10
ABIGAIL
Say, knave, why rail'st upon my father thus?
ITHAMORE
Oh, my master has the bravest policy.
ABIGAIL
Wherein?
ITHAMORE
Why, know you not?
ABIGAIL
Why no.   15
ITHAMORE
Know you not of Mathias' and Don Lodowick's disaster?
ABIGAIL
No, what was it?
ITHAMORE
Why the devil invented a challenge, my master writ it, and
I carried it, first to Lodowick, and *imprimis* to Mathias.
And then they met, and as the story says,   20
In doleful wise they ended both their days.
ABIGAIL
And was my father furtherer of their deaths?
ITHAMORE
Am I Ithamore?
ABIGAIL
Yes.
ITHAMORE
So sure did your father write, and I carry the challenge.   25

9, 12 *bravest* finest
19 *imprimis* (Latin) first [Ithamore's error]
20 *met, and as* ed. (Q met, as)
22 *furtherer* the contriver

ABIGAIL

  Well, Ithamore, let me request thee this,
  Go to the new-made nunnery, and inquire
  For any of the friars of St. Jaques,
  And say, I pray them come and speak with me.

ITHAMORE

  I pray, mistress, will you answer me to one question?   30

ABIGAIL

  Well, sirrah, what is't?

ITHAMORE

  A very feeling one; have not the nuns fine sport with the
  friars now and then?

ABIGAIL

  Go to, sirrah sauce, is this your question? Get ye gone.

ITHAMORE

  I will forsooth, mistress.   35

                                Exit

ABIGAIL

  Hard-hearted father, unkind Barabas,
  Was this the pursuit of thy policy?
  To make me show them favour severally,
  That by my favour they should both be slain?
  Admit thou lov'dst not Lodowick for his sire,   40
  Yet Don Mathias ne'er offended thee:
  But thou wert set upon extreme revenge,
  Because the Governor dispossessed thee once,
  And couldst not venge it, but upon his son,
  Nor on his son, but by Mathias' means;   45
  Nor on Mathias, but by murdering me.
  But I perceive there is no love on earth,
  Pity in Jews, nor piety in Turks.
  But here comes cursed Ithamore with the friar.

                Enter ITHAMORE, FRIAR

FRIAR

  Virgo, salve.   50

ITHAMORE

  When, duck you?

28 *Jaques* ed. (Q Iaynes) (pronounce 'a' as in 'makes')
34 *go to, sirrah sauce* get away, you saucy fellow
37 *pursuit* aim
40 *sire* ed. (Q sinne)
43 *Governor* ed. (Q Pryor)
50 *Virgo, salve* (Latin) Greetings, maiden
51 *When, duck you?* What, are you bowing and scraping?

ABIGAIL

Welcome grave friar: Ithamore begone.

Exit [ITHAMORE]

Know, holy sir, I am bold to solicit thee.

FRIAR

Wherein?

ABIGAIL

To get me be admitted for a nun.   55

FRIAR

Why Abigail it is not yet long since
That I did labour thy admission,
And then thou didst not like that holy life.

ABIGAIL

Then were my thoughts so frail and unconfirmed,
And I was chained to follies of the world: 60
But now experience, purchasèd with grief,
Has made me see the difference of things.
My sinful soul, alas, hath paced too long
The fatal labyrinth of misbelief,
Far from the sun that gives eternal life.   65

FRIAR

Who taught thee this?

ABIGAIL

The abbess of the house,
Whose zealous admonition I embrace:
Oh therefore, Jacomo, let me be one,
Although unworthy, of that sisterhood.   70

FRIAR

Abigail I will, but see thou change no more,
For that will be most heavy to thy soul.

ABIGAIL

That was my father's fault.

FRIAR

Thy father's, how?

ABIGAIL

Nay, you shall pardon me: [*aside*] oh Barabas,   75
Though thou deservest hardly at my hands,
Yet never shall these lips bewray thy life.

55 *get me be admitted for* procure my admission as
59 *unconfirmed* unsettled
65 *sun* ed. (Q Sonne)
68 *admonition* counsel
69 *Jacomo* ed. (Q *Iacomi*)
70 *unworthy, of* ed. (Q unworthy of)
77 *bewray* betray

FRIAR
  Come, shall we go?
ABIGAIL
  My duty waits on you.

                                    Exeunt

[Act III, Scene iv]

Enter BARABAS *reading a letter*

BARABAS
  What, Abigail become a nun again?
  False, and unkind; what, hast thou lost thy father?
  And all unknown, and unconstrained of me,
  Art thou again got to the nunnery?
  Now here she writes, and wills me to repent.   5
  Repentance? *Spurca*: what pretendeth this?
  I fear she knows ('tis so) of my device
  In Don Mathias' and Lodovico's deaths:
  If so, 'tis time that it be seen into:
  For she that varies from me in belief   10
  Gives great presumption that she loves me not;
  Or loving, doth dislike of something done.
  But who comes here?

             [Enter ITHAMORE]

        Oh Ithamore come near;
  Come near my love, come near thy master's life,
  My trusty servant, nay, my second self;   15
  For I have now no hope but even in thee;
  And on that hope my happiness is built:
  When saw'st thou Abigail?
ITHAMORE
  Today.
BARABAS
  With whom?   20
ITHAMORE
  A friar.

  2 *unkind* unnatural
  2 *lost* abandoned
  6 *Spurca* (Italian) 'filthy [repentance]', i.e. 'I scorn it'
  6 *pretendeth* means
 11 *presumption* grounds for belief
 15 *self* ed. (Q life)

BARABAS

A friar? false villain, he hath done the deed.

ITHAMORE

How sir?

BARABAS

Why made mine Abigail a nun.

ITHAMORE

That's no lie, for she sent me for him.   25

BARABAS

O unhappy day,
False, credulous, inconstant Abigail!
But let 'em go: and Ithamore, from hence
Ne'er shall she grieve me more with her disgrace;
Ne'er shall she live to inherit aught of mine,   30
Be blest of me, nor come within my gates,
But perish underneath my bitter curse,
Like Cain by Adam, for his brother's death.

ITHAMORE

Oh master.

BARABAS

Ithamore, intreat not for her, I am moved,   35
And she is hateful to my soul and me:
And 'less thou yield to this that I intreat,
I cannot think but that thou hat'st my life.

ITHAMORE

Who I, master? Why I'll run to some rock and throw
myself headlong into the sea; why I'll do anything for your   40
sweet sake.

BARABAS

Oh trusty Ithamore; no servant, but my friend;
I here adopt thee for mine only heir,
All that I have is thine when I am dead,
And whilst I live use half; spend as myself;   45
Here take my keys, I'll give 'em thee anon:
Go buy thee garments: but thou shalt not want:
Only know this, that thus thou art to do:
But first go fetch me in the pot of rice
That for our supper stands upon the fire.   50

37 *'less* ed. (Q least)

39–41 Q prints these lines as prose with capitals at the beginning of lines
('Throw', 'Thing'). Editors make it into three lines of verse ending at
'rock', 'sea' and 'sake'. But only the last of these is a convincing line of
verse, and as Ithamore speaks prose in the rest of the scene (except for
his rhymed exit) I have left the passage as prose.

ITHAMORE
  I hold my head my master's hungry: I go sir.

                                                                    Exit

BARABAS
  Thus every villain ambles after wealth
  Although he ne'er be richer than in hope:
  But husht.

                    Enter ITHAMORE *with the pot*

ITHAMORE
  Here 'tis, master.   55
BARABAS
  Well said, Ithamore; what, hast thou brought the ladle with
  thee too?
ITHAMORE
  Yes, sir, the proverb says, he that eats with the devil had
  need of a long spoon, I have brought you a ladle.
BARABAS
  Very well, Ithamore, then now be secret: 60
  And for thy sake, whom I so dearly love,
  Now shalt thou see the death of Abigail,
  That thou mayst freely live to be my heir.
ITHAMORE
  Why, master, will you poison her with a mess of rice
  porridge that will preserve life, make her round and plump,   65
  and batten more than you are aware?
BARABAS
  Ay, but Ithamore seest thou this?
  It is a precious powder that I bought
  Of an Italian in Ancona once,
  Whose operation is to bind, infect,   70
  And poison deeply: yet not appear
  In forty hours after it is ta'en.
ITHAMORE
  How master?
BARABAS
  Thus Ithamore:
  This even they use in Malta here ('tis called   75
  Saint Jaques' even) and then I say they use

---

51 *hold* bet, wager
52 *ambles* paces steadily
54 *husht* ed. (Q hush't) whist, silence
66 *batten* grow fat
75 *even* evening
76 *Jaques'* ed. (Q *Iagues*) (two syllables)

To send their alms unto the nunneries:
Among the rest bear this, and set it there;
There's a dark entry where they take it in,
Where they must neither see the messenger,   80
Nor make inquiry who hath sent it them.

ITHAMORE
How so?

BARABAS
Belike there is some ceremony in't.
There Ithamore must thou go place this pot:
Stay, let me spice it first.   85

ITHAMORE
Pray do, and let me help you master. Pray let me taste first.

BARABAS
Prithee do: what say'st thou now?

ITHAMORE
Troth master, I'm loath such a pot of pottage should be
spoiled.

BARABAS
Peace, Ithamore, 'tis better so than spared.   90
Assure thyself thou shalt have broth by the eye.
My purse, my coffer, and my self is thine.

ITHAMORE
Well, master, I go.

BARABAS
Stay, first let me stir it Ithamore.
As fatal be it to her as the draught   95
Of which great Alexander drunk, and died:
And with her let it work like Borgia's wine,
Whereof his sire, the Pope, was poisonèd.
In few, the blood of Hydra, Lerna's bane,
The juice of hebon, and Cocytus' breath,   100
And all the poisons of the Stygian pool,
Break from the fiery kingdom; and in this
Vomit your venom, and invenom her
That like a fiend hath left her father thus.

---

84 *pot* ed. (Q plot)
91 *by the eye* in plenty
99 *Lerna's bane* which was the plague of Lerna
101 *hebon* a poisonous plant, henbane or yew

---

96 *great Alexander*. Alexander the Great contracted his fatal illness after a
drinking-bout.
98 *the Pope*. Alexander VI (died 1503, actually of malaria), father of
Cesare Borgia.

ITHAMORE
   What a blessing has he given't! Was ever pot of rice porridge   105
   so sauced? What shall I do with it?
BARABAS
   Oh my sweet Ithamore go set it down
   And come again so soon as thou hast done,
   For I have other business for thee.
ITHAMORE
   Here's a drench to poison a whole stable of Flanders mares: 110
   I'll carry't to the nuns with a powder.
BARABAS
   And the horse pestilence to boot; away.
ITHAMORE
   I am gone.
   Pay me my wages for my work is done.

                                            Exit

BARABAS
   I'll pay thee with a vengeance Ithamore.   115
                                          Exit

[Act III, Scene v]

Enter GOVERNOR, [MARTIN DEL] BOSCO, KNIGHTS, [*meeting a*]
BASSO

GOVERNOR
   Welcome great Basso, how fares Calymath,
   What wind drives you thus into Malta road?
BASSO
   The wind that bloweth all the world besides,
   Desire of gold.

---

110 *drench* dose
112 *to boot* too, into the bargain
  1 *Basso* ed. (Q *Bashaws*; and uses that spelling from this point)

---

111 *with a powder*. Meaningless. Spencer's explanation 'in haste. With an
    obvious pun' is unsatisfactory: the Oxford English Dictionary gives
    'powder' as a colloquial verb meaning 'rush' (first in 1632) but no noun-
    phrase from it. Case (quoted by Bennett) conjectures 'with a pox',
    which 'would explain Barabas's supplementary remark, suggested by
    "a whole stable", etc.'.
  2 Some editors smooth the verse by reading 'thus drives you': but the
    stress on 'you' is deliberate, and expresses the Governor's feigned
    surprise (he having resolved to pay no tribute) at the Turks' arrival; *cf.*
    his next speech. The Governor's self-confidence makes him dramatically
    attractive in this short scene.

GOVERNOR

Desire of gold, great sir?   5
That's to be gotten in the Western Ind:
In Malta are no golden minerals.

BASSO

To you of Malta thus saith Calymath:
The time you took for respite, is at hand,
For the performance of your promise past;   10
And for the tribute-money I am sent.

GOVERNOR

Basso, in brief, shalt have no tribute here,
Nor shall the heathens live upon our spoil:
First will we race the city walls ourselves,
Lay waste the island, hew the temples down,   15
And shipping off our goods to Sicily,
Open an entrance for the wasteful sea,
Whose billows beating the resistless banks,
Shall overflow it with their refluence.

BASSO

Well, Governor, since thou hast broke the league   20
By flat denial of the promised tribute,
Talk not of racing down your city walls,
You shall not need trouble yourselves so far,
For Selim-Calymath shall come himself,
And with brass bullets batter down your towers,   25
And turn proud Malta to a wilderness,
For these intolerable wrongs of yours;
And so farewell.

[Exit]

GOVERNOR

Farewell.
And now you men of Malta look about,   30
And let's provide to welcome Calymath:
Close your portcullis, charge your basilisks,
And as you profitably take up arms,
So now courageously encounter them;
For by this answer, broken is the league,   35
And nought is to be looked for now but wars,
And nought to us more welcome is than wars.

Exeunt

14 *race* raze, level with the ground
16 *off* ed. (Q of)
17 *wasteful* destroying
18 *resistless* unresisting
19 *refluence* flowing back
32 *basilisks* brass cannons

[Act III, Scene vi]

[Enter the TWO FRIARS]

1 FRIAR
  Oh brother, brother, all the nuns are sick,
  And physic will not help them; they must die.
2 FRIAR
  The abbess sent for me to be confessed:
  Oh what a sad confession will there be!
1 FRIAR
  And so did fair Maria send for me: 5
  I'll to her lodging; hereabouts she lies.

                                                          Exit

                    Enter ABIGAIL

2 FRIAR
  What, all dead save only Abigail?
ABIGAIL
  And I shall die too, for I feel death coming.
  Where is the friar that conversed with me?
2 FRIAR
  Oh he is gone to see the other nuns.   10
ABIGAIL
  I sent for him, but seeing you are come,
  Be you my ghostly father; and first know
  That in this house I lived religiously,
  Chaste, and devout, much sorrowing for my sins;
  But ere I came—   15
2 FRIAR
  What then?
ABIGAIL
  I did offend high heaven so grievously,
  As I am almost desperate for my sins:
  And one offence torments me more than all.
  You knew Mathias and Don Lodowick?   20
2 FRIAR
  Yes, what of them?

    III.vi. s.d. ed. (Q *Enter two Fryars and Abigall.*
  18 *desperate* despairing of heavenly forgiveness

ABIGAIL

My father did contract me to 'em both:
First to Don Lodowick, him I never loved;
Mathias was the man that I held dear,
And for his sake did I become a nun.   25

2 FRIAR

So, say how was their end?

ABIGAIL

Both jealous of my love, envied each other:
And by my father's practice, which is there
Set down at large, the gallants were both slain.

                              [Gives him a paper]

2 FRIAR

Oh monstrous villainy!   30

ABIGAIL

To work my peace, this I confess to thee;
Reveal it not, for then my father dies.

2 FRIAR

Know that confession must not be revealed,
The canon law forbids it, and the priest
That makes it known, being degraded first,   35
Shall be condemned, and then sent to the fire.

ABIGAIL

So I have heard; pray therefore keep it close.
Death seizeth on my heart, ah gentle friar
Convert my father that he may be saved,
And witness that I die a Christian.   40

                                        [Dies]

2 FRIAR

Ay, and a virgin too, that grieves me most:
But I must to the Jew and exclaim on him,
And make him stand in fear of me.

                    Enter 1 FRIAR

1 FRIAR

Oh brother, all the nuns are dead, let's bury them.

22 *contract* betroth
27 *envied* (stress second syllable) hated
28 *practice* contrivance, treachery
37 *close* secret
42, 46 *exclaim on, against* denounce

40–1 An astonishing juxtaposition of pathos and coarseness, effectively
    blackening the Friar's character in readiness for his negotiations with
    Barabas in the next scene.

2 FRIAR

First help to bury this, then go with me　　　45
And help me to exclaim against the Jew.

1 FRIAR

Why? what has he done?

2 FRIAR

A thing that makes me tremble to unfold.

1 FRIAR

What, has he crucified a child?

2 FRIAR

No, but a worse thing: 'twas told me in shrift;　　　50
Thou know'st 'tis death and if it be revealed.
Come let's away.

Exeunt [with the body]

Act IV [Scene i]

Enter BARABAS, ITHAMORE.　*Bells within*

BARABAS

There is no music to a Christian's knell:
How sweet the bells ring now the nuns are dead,
That sound at other times like tinkers' pans!
I was afraid the poison had not wrought;
Or though it wrought, it would have done no good,　　　5
For every year they swell, and yet they live;
Now all are dead, not one remains alive.

ITHAMORE

That's brave, master, but think you it will not be known?

BARABAS

How can it if we two be secret?

ITHAMORE

For my part fear you not.　　　10

BARABAS

I'd cut thy throat if I did.

ITHAMORE

And reason too;
But here's a royal monastery hard by,
Good master let me poison all the monks.

BARABAS

Thou shalt not need, for now the nuns are dead,　　　15
They'll die with grief.

---

1 *to* equal to
6 *swell* i.e. are pregnant

ITHAMORE
Do you not sorrow for your daughter's death?
BARABAS
No, but I grieve because she lived so long;
An Hebrew born, and would become a Christian.
Catso, diabole!   20

Enter the TWO FRIARS

ITHAMORE
Look, look, master, here come two religious caterpillars.
BARABAS
I smelt 'em ere they came.
ITHAMORE
God-a-mercy nose; come let's begone.
2 FRIAR
Stay wicked Jew, repent, I say, and stay.
1 FRIAR
Thou hast offended, therefore must be damned.   25
BARABAS
I fear they know we sent the poisoned broth.
ITHAMORE
And so do I, master, therefore speak 'em fair.
2 FRIAR
Barabas, thou hast—
1 FRIAR
Ay, that thou hast—
BARABAS
True, I have money, what though I have?   30
2 FRIAR
Thou art a—
1 FRIAR
Ay, that thou art, a—
BARABAS
What needs all this? I know I am a Jew.
2 FRIAR
Thy daughter—

18–19 *so long;/An* ed. (Q so long an)
20 *Catso, diabole!* (Q [marginally] *Catho diabola:*) foreign oaths (from
   Italian *cazzo*, penis, and Spanish *diablo*, devil)
21 *caterpillars* parasites
23 *God-a-mercy nose* Thanks to your big nose
32 *art, a* ed. (Q art a)

30–41 Barabas's method here, of forestalling the Friars, recalls his wilful
   misunderstanding of the Governor in I.ii. He briefly reverts to it at
   line 80.

1 FRIAR
Ay, thy daughter—   35
BARABAS
Oh speak not of her, then I die with grief.
2 FRIAR
Remember that—
1 FRIAR
Ay, remember that—
BARABAS
I must needs say that I have been a great usurer.
2 FRIAR
Thou hast committed—   40
BARABAS
Fornication? but that was in another country: and besides,
the wench is dead.
2 FRIAR
Ay, but Barabas remember Mathias and Don Lodowick.
BARABAS
Why, what of them?
2 FRIAR
I will not say that by a forged challenge they met.   45
BARABAS [*aside to Ithamore*]
She has confessed, and we are both undone,
My bosom inmate; but I must dissemble.—
Oh holy friars, the burthen of my sins
Lie heavy on my soul; then pray you tell me,
Is't not too late now to turn Christian?   50
I have been zealous in the Jewish faith,
Hard-hearted to the poor, a covetous wretch,
That would for lucre's sake have sold my soul.
A hundred for a hundred I have ta'en;
And now for store of wealth may I compare   55

46–7 *undone,/My bosom inmate;* ed. (Q vndone;/My bosome inmates,)
54 *A hundred for a hundred* interest at a hundred per cent.

46–47 Q prints *but I must dissemble* in italics, and has *aside* marginally, but
clearly the lines are both 'aside' in the sense that the Friars do not hear
them. The phrase 'My bosome inmates' (Q) has been taken as an ex-
clamation (i.e. 'The friars are now in my secrets'–Spencer), but this
seems too cryptic for dramatic speech. It might be defended as the beginning of Barabas's address to the Friars, but this would be out of
place *before* an aside. When the emendation 'inmate' is made, Bennett
takes it as referring to Abigail. More probably, however, as Dyce thinks,
it continues line 46 and is addressed to Ithamore, whom Barabas has
already flattered as 'my love, . . . my second self' (III.iv, 14–15). This
would be easy to present on stage, Barabas turning from the Friars to
Ithamore, and then, with 'but I must dissemble', turning back to the
Friars.

With all the Jews in Malta; but what is wealth?
I am a Jew, and therefore am I lost.
Would penance serve to atone for this my sin,
I could afford to whip myself to death.

ITHAMORE

And so could I; but penance will not serve.   60

BARABAS

To fast, to pray, and wear a shirt of hair,
And on my knees creep to Jerusalem.
Cellars of wine, and sollars full of wheat,
Warehouses stuffed with spices and with drugs,
Whole chests of gold, in bullion and in coin,   65
Besides I know not how much weight in pearl
Orient and round, have I within my house;
At Alexandria, merchandise unsold:
But yesterday two ships went from this town,
Their voyage will be worth ten thousand crowns.   70
In Florence, Venice, Antwerp, London, Seville,
Frankfort, Lubeck, Moscow, and where not,
Have I debts owing; and in most of these,
Great sums of money lying in the banco;
All this I'll give to some religious house   75
So I may be baptized and live therein.

1 FRIAR

Oh good Barabas come to our house.

2 FRIAR

Oh no, good Barabas come to our house.
And Barabas, you know—

BARABAS

I know that I have highly sinned,   80
You shall convert me, you shall have all my wealth.

1 FRIAR

Oh Barabas, their laws are strict.

BARABAS

I know they are, and I will be with you.

2 FRIAR

They wear no shirts, and they go barefoot too.

BARABAS

Then 'tis not for me; and I am resolved   85

58 *serve to atone* ed. (Q serue)
63 *sollars* lofts
65 *bullion* ed. (Q *Bulloine* i.e. Boulogne)
67 *Orient* precious (genuine Eastern)
74 *banco* bank
84 *2 Friar* ed. (Q 1.)

You shall confess me, and have all my goods.

1 FRIAR

Good Barabas come to me.

BARABAS

You see I answer him, and yet he stays;

Rid him away, and go you home with me.

1 FRIAR

I'll be with you tonight.   90

BARABAS

Come to my house at one o'clock this night.

1 FRIAR

You hear your answer, and you may be gone.

2 FRIAR

Why go get you away.

1 FRIAR

I will not go for thee.

2 FRIAR

Not, then I'll make thee rogue.   95

1 FRIAR

How, dost call me rogue?

Fight

ITHAMORE

Part 'em, master, part 'em.

90 *1 Friar* ed. (Q 2.)
95 *rogue* ed. (Q goe)

82–96 The assignment of the Friars' speeches here is a vexed question.
Clearly line 90 ('I'll be with you tonight') belongs to 1 Friar, in view of
the sequel (lines 156–8): editors vary in their assignment of other
speeches. Maxwell (*Modern Language Review*, XLIII, 1948) argues that
line 84 is rightly given by Q to 1 Friar, who refuses to take 'yes' for an
answer, and harps on the hardships of 2 Friar's house. But this view
overlooks Barabas's lines 103–5, which make it plain that 2 Friar has
abused 1 Friar's house too; it also misses the farcical stage-effect of
Barabas consciously playing the weathercock between the two Friars.
Maxwell suggests that Barabas does not allow either Friar to hear what
he says to the other, but I think he replies aloud to both, deliberately
wavering so that they angrily try to outbid each other, until line 88
when he speaks privately to 2 Friar (having 'answered' 1 Friar by
accepting 2 Friar's offer). He then replies aloud to 1 Friar's self-
invitation, with a line (91) which 1 Friar takes for an agreement to be
converted and hence an 'answer' to 2 Friar, but which 2 Friar takes
as merely putting off 1 Friar until after 2 Friar has converted Barabas.
Therefore each Friar thinks that the other should go away. Barabas
continues to play this double game. He reassures 2 Friar that he can
handle 1 Friar in his absence (100), and reassures 1 Friar that he will
merely fob off 2 Friar at home (102 – with conscious irony, as he intends
his death; the irony is continued in lines 106–8).

BARABAS

This is mere frailty, brethren, be content.
Friar Barnardine go you with Ithamore.
You know my mind, let me alone with him.   100

1 FRIAR

Why does he go to thy house, let him begone.

BARABAS

I'll give him something and so stop his mouth.

                                [Exeunt ITHAMORE *and* 2 FRIAR]

I never heard of any man but he
Maligned the order of the Jacobins:
But do you think that I believe his words?   105
Why brother you converted Abigail;
And I am bound in charity to requite it,
And so I will, oh Jacomo, fail not but come.

1 FRIAR

But Barabas who shall be your godfathers?
For presently you shall be shrived.   110

BARABAS

Marry the Turk shall be one of my godfathers,
But not a word to any of your covent.

1 FRIAR

I warrant thee, Barabas.

                                          Exit

BARABAS

So now the fear is past, and I am safe:
For he that shrived her is within my house.   115
What if I murdered him ere Jacomo comes?
Now I have such a plot for both their lives,
As never Jew nor Christian knew the like:
One turned my daughter, therefore he shall die;
The other knows enough to have my life,   120
Therefore 'tis not requisite he should live.
But are not both these wise men to suppose
That I will leave my house, my goods, and all,

100 Q adds prefix *Ith.*, and omits prefix of next speech
102 s.d. ed. (Q *Exit.*)
112 *covent* convent, community
119 *turned* converted

---

104 *Jacobins.* Dominican Friars (so called in France because their first house
in Paris was in the Rue St. Jacques). They wore a black mantle over a
white habit, and were called Black Friars, as distinct from the Francis-
cans or Grey Friars. Both orders were vowed to corporate poverty and
lived by begging.

To fast and be well whipped; I'll none of that.
Now Friar Barnardine I come to you,   125
I'll feast you, lodge you, give you fair words,
And after that, I and my trusty Turk—
No more but so: it must and shall be done.
Ithamore, tell me, is the friar asleep?

Enter ITHAMORE

ITHAMORE
Yes; and I know not what the reason is: 130
Do what I can he will not strip himself,
Nor go to bed, but sleeps in his own clothes;
I fear me he mistrusts what we intend.
BARABAS
No, 'tis an order which the friars use:
Yet if he knew our meanings, could he scape?   135
ITHAMORE
No, none can hear him, cry he ne'er so loud.
BARABAS
Why true, therefore did I place him there:
The other chambers open towards the street.
ITHAMORE
You loiter, master, wherefore stay we thus?
Oh how I long to see him shake his heels.   140
BARABAS
Come on, sirrah,
Off with your girdle, make a handsome noose;
Friar, awake.
2 FRIAR
What, do you mean to strangle me?
ITHAMORE
Yes, 'cause you use to confess.   145

133 *mistrusts* suspects
134 *order* rule, custom
135 *meanings* intentions
145 *use to confess* make a practice of hearing confession

---

129 Here some editors begin a new scene; but Barabas's soliloquy marks a
suspension of dramatic time, and it is now supposed to be much later
that evening. Marlowe does not trouble about verisimilitude in these
matters. Notice also that Ithamore twice refers to a pre-arranged plan to
strangle the Friar, though in fact the plan has just been formed in
Barabas's soliloquy (117–18); and that at line 153 the propping up of the
Friar's body is presented as Ithamore's invention, though it must have
been included in Barabas's plan. These inconsistencies would pass in
the excitement of performance.

BARABAS
Blame not us but the proverb, confess and be hanged. Pull
hard.

2 FRIAR
What, will you have my life?

BARABAS
Pull hard, I say, you would have had my goods.

ITHAMORE
Ay, and our lives too, therefore pull amain. 150
'Tis neatly done, sir, here's no print at all.

BARABAS
Then is it as it should be, take him up.

ITHAMORE
Nay, master, be ruled by me a little; so, let him lean upon
his staff; excellent, he stands as if he were begging of bacon.

BARABAS
Who would not think but that this friar lived? 155
What time o' night is't now, sweet Ithamore?

ITHAMORE
Towards one.

Enter 1 FRIAR

BARABAS
Then will not Jacomo be long from hence.
[*Exeunt* BARABAS *and* ITHAMORE]

1 FRIAR
This is the hour
Wherein I shall proceed; oh happy hour, 160
Wherein I shall convert an infidel,
And bring his gold into our treasury.
But soft, is not this Barnardine? It is:
And understanding I should come this way,
Stands here o' purpose, meaning me some wrong, 165
And intercept my going to the Jew;
Barnardine;

148 *have* ed. (Q saue)
150 *amain* strongly
157 s.d. ed. (Q *Enter Iocoma*; his speeches are headed *Ioco*.)
160 *proceed* do well, be lucky

158 *Exeunt.* Again a new scene in some editions; but the placing of 1 Friar's
entrance shows that the action is continuous. The Friar appears before
Barabas and Ithamore withdraw: they only just get out of sight in time.

Wilt thou not speak? Thou think'st I see thee not;
Away, I'd wish thee, and let me go by:
No, wilt thou not? Nay then I'll force my way;   170
And see, a staff stands ready for the purpose:
As thou lik'st that, stop me another time.

     Strike him, he falls. Enter BARABAS [*and* ITHAMORE]

BARABAS
Why how now Jacomo, what hast thou done?
1 FRIAR
Why stricken him that would have struck at me.
BARABAS
Who is it, Barnardine? Now out alas, he's slain.   175
ITHAMORE
Ay, master, he's slain; look how his brains drop out on's nose.
1 FRIAR
Good sirs I have done't, but nobody knows it but you two, I
may escape.
BARABAS
So might my man and I hang with you for company.
ITHAMORE
No, let us bear him to the magistrates.   180
1 FRIAR
Good Barabas let me go.
BARABAS
No, pardon me, the law must have his course.
I must be forced to give in evidence,
That being importuned by this Barnardine
To be a Christian, I shut him out,   185
And there he sate: now I to keep my word,
And give my goods and substance to your house,
Was up thus early; with intent to go
Unto your friary, because you stayed.
ITHAMORE
Fie upon 'em, master, will you turn Christian, when holy   190
friars turn devils and murder one another?

176 *on's* of his
189 *stayed* were late in coming

---

171 Not 2 Friar's staff, on which his body was leaning: 1 Friar could hardly
say that it stood ready for his purpose, nor take it without dislodging
the body. This is evidently another staff, left conveniently on stage by
Barabas. It is true that he did not say he was leaving it; but if he had
done so, he would have spoiled the surprise of his plan by letting the
audience guess it too soon.

BARABAS

No, for this example I'll remain a Jew:
Heaven bless me; what, a friar a murderer?
When shall you see a Jew commit the like?

ITHAMORE

Why a Turk could ha' done no more.   195

BARABAS

Tomorrow is the sessions; you shall to it.
Come Ithamore, let's help to take him hence.

1 FRIAR

Villains, I am a sacred person, touch me not.

BARABAS

The law shall touch you, we'll but lead you, we:
'Las I could weep at your calamity.   200
Take in the staff too, for that must be shown:
Law wills that each particular be known.

Exeunt

[Act IV, Scene ii]

Enter COURTESAN *and* PILIA-BORZA

COURTESAN

Pilia-Borza, didst thou meet with Ithamore?

PILIA-BORZA

I did.

COURTESAN

And didst thou deliver my letter?

PILIA-BORZA

I did.

COURTESAN

And what think'st thou, will he come?   5

PILIA-BORZA

I think so, and yet I cannot tell, for at the reading of the
letter, he looked like a man of another world.

COURTESAN

Why so?

PILIA-BORZA

That such a base slave as he should be saluted by such a tall
man as I am, from such a beautiful dame as you.   10

COURTESAN

And what said he?

200 *'Las* alas
202 *wills* requires
202 *particular* detail

PILIA-BORZA

Not a wise word, only gave me a nod, as who should say,
Is it even so? And so I left him, being driven to a non-plus
at the critical aspect of my terrible countenance.

COURTESAN

And where didst meet him?   15

PILIA-BORZA

Upon mine own freehold within forty foot of the gallows,
conning his neck-verse I take it, looking of a friar's execution,
whom I saluted with an old hempen proverb, *Hodie tibi, cras
mihi*, and so I left him to the mercy of the hangman: but the
exercise being done, see where he comes.   20

Enter ITHAMORE

ITHAMORE

I never knew a man take his death so patiently as this friar;
he was ready to leap off ere the halter was about his neck:
and when the hangman had put on his hempen tippet, he
made such haste to his prayers, as if he had had another cure
to serve; well, go whither he will, I'll be none of his followers   25
in haste. And now I think on't, going to the execution, a
fellow met me with a muschatoes like a raven's wing, and a
dagger with a hilt like a warming-pan, and he gave me a letter
from one Madam Bellamira, saluting me in such sort as if
he had meant to make clean my boots with his lips; the   30
effect was, that I should come to her house, I wonder what
the reason is; it may be she sees more in me than I can find
in myself: for she writes further, that she loves me ever since
she saw me, and who would not requite such love? Here's
her house, and here she comes, and now would I were gone,   35
I am not worthy to look upon her.

---

13 *driven to a non-plus* nonplussed, dumbstruck
14 *critical aspect* (astrological) sinister influence
16 *freehold* personal land (i.e. where he picks pockets for his living)
17 *conning* studying
18 *whom* i.e. the friar
18–19 *Hodie tibi, cras mihi* (Latin) today your [fortune], tomorrow mine
20 *exercise being done* service being over
23 *tippet* scarf (i.e. noose)
24–5 *cure to serve* parish to minister to
27 *muschatoes* moustache

---

17 *neck-verse*. The verse read by a criminal to entitle him to benefit of
clergy. Here probably used figuratively to mean that Ithamore was
getting experience for his own execution.

PILIA-BORZA
This is the gentleman you writ to.

ITHAMORE [*aside*]
Gentleman, he flouts me, what gentry can be in a poor Turk of ten pence? I'll be gone.

COURTESAN
Is't not a sweet-faced youth, Pilia-Borza?   40

ITHAMORE [*aside*]
Again, sweet youth;—Did not you, sir, bring the sweet youth a letter?

PILIA-BORZA
I did sir, and from this gentlewoman, who as myself, and the rest of the family, stand or fall at your service.

COURTESAN
Though woman's modesty should hale me back,   45
I can withhold no longer; welcome sweet love.

ITHAMORE [*aside*]
Now am I clean, or rather foully out of the way.

COURTESAN
Whither so soon?

ITHAMORE [*aside*]
I'll go steal some money from my master to make me handsome.—Pray pardon me, I must go see a ship discharged.   50

COURTESAN
Canst thou be so unkind to leave me thus?

PILIA-BORZA
And ye did but know how she loves you, sir—

ITHAMORE
Nay, I care not how much she loves me; sweet Allamira, would I had my master's wealth for thy sake.

PILIA-BORZA
And you can have it, sir, and if you please.   55

ITHAMORE
If 'twere above ground I could, and would have it; but he hides and buries it up as partridges do their eggs, under the earth.

PILIA-BORZA
And is't not possible to find it out?

38 *flouts* mocks
40 *Pilia-Borza?* ed. (Q *Pilia?*)
44 *family* household
47 *clean* completely
50 *discharged* unloaded
52 *sir*— ed. (Q *Sir.*)
53 *Allamira* Ithamore's error for Bellamira

ITHAMORE
By no means possible.   60
COURTESAN [aside]
What shall we do with this base villain then?
PILIA-BORZA [aside]
Let me alone, do but you speak him fair:—
But you know some secrets of the Jew, which if they were
revealed, would do him harm.
ITHAMORE
Ay, and such as— Go to, no more, I'll make him send me half   65
he has, and glad he scapes so too. Pen and ink:
I'll write unto him, we'll have money straight.
PILIA-BORZA
Send for a hundred crowns at least.
ITHAMORE
Ten hundred thousand crowns. (He writes) 'Master
Barabas—'   70
PILIA-BORZA
Write not so submissively, but threatening him.
ITHAMORE
'Sirrah Barabas, send me a hundred crowns.'
PILIA-BORZA
Put in two hundred at least.
ITHAMORE
'I charge thee send me three hundred by this bearer, and
this shall be your warrant; if you do not, no more but so.'   75
PILIA-BORZA
Tell him you will confess.
ITHAMORE
'Otherwise I'll confess all.' Vanish and return in a twinkle.
PILIA-BORZA
Let me alone, I'll use him in his kind.

                                                      [Exit]
ITHAMORE
Hang him Jew.
COURTESAN
Now, gentle Ithamore, lie in my lap.   80
Where are my maids? Provide a running banquet;

---

78 *in his kind* according to his nature, i.e. as he deserves
81 *running banquet* banquet quickly prepared

---

69 *He writes.* Ithamore here takes up his pen, and begins dictating to himself (thus allowing Pilia-Borza to improve on his letter before he writes
it down). 'No more but so' is a vague threat, for which Pilia-Borza
substitutes a precise threat.

Send to the merchant, bid him bring me silks,
Shall Ithamore my love go in such rags?
ITHAMORE
And bid the jeweller come hither too.
COURTESAN
I have no husband, sweet, I'll marry thee.   85
ITHAMORE
Content, but we will leave this paltry land,
And sail from hence to Greece, to lovely Greece,
I'll be thy Jason, thou my golden fleece;
Where painted carpets o'er the meads are hurled,
And Bacchus' vineyards over-spread the world: 90
Where woods and forests go in goodly green,
I'll be Adonis, thou shalt be Love's Queen.
The meads, the orchards, and the primrose lanes,
Instead of sedge and reed, bear sugar canes:
Thou in those groves, by Dis above,   95
Shalt live with me and be my love.
COURTESAN
Whither will I not go with gentle Ithamore?

Enter PILIA-BORZA

ITHAMORE
How now? hast thou the gold?
PILIA-BORZA
Yes.
ITHAMORE
But came it freely, did the cow give down her milk freely?   100
PILIA-BORZA
At reading of the letter, he stared and stamped, and turned
aside, I took him by the beard, and looked upon him thus;
told him he were best to send it, then he hugged and
embraced me.
ITHAMORE
Rather for fear than love.   105
PILIA-BORZA
Then like a Jew he laughed and jeered, and told me he loved

90 *over-spread* ed. (Q ore-spread)
95 *Dis* Pluto   102 *beard* ed. (Q sterd)

---

96 Alluding to Marlowe's lyric *The Passionate Shepherd to his Love*, which
     ends thus:
> The shepherd swains shall dance and sing
> For thy delight each May-morning.
> If these delights thy mind may move,
> Then live with me, and be my love.

me for your sake, and said what a faithful servant you had
been.

ITHAMORE

The more villain he to keep me thus: here's goodly 'parel,
is there not?   110

PILIA-BORZA

To conclude, he gave me ten crowns.

ITHAMORE

But ten? I'll not leave him worth a grey groat, give me a
ream of paper, we'll have a kingdom of gold for't.

PILIA-BORZA

Write for five hundred crowns.

ITHAMORE [*writes*]

'Sirrah Jew, as you love your life send me five hundred   115
crowns, and give the bearer a hundred.' Tell him I must
have't.

PILIA-BORZA

I warrant your worship shall have't.

ITHAMORE

And if he ask why I demand so much, tell him, I scorn to
write a line under a hundred crowns.   120

PILIA-BORZA

You'd make a rich poet, sir. I am gone.

                                                                                          Exit

ITHAMORE

Take thou the money, spend it for my sake.

COURTESAN

'Tis not thy money, but thy self I weigh:
Thus Bellamira esteems of gold;

                                                              [*Throws it aside*]

But thus of thee.   125

                                                                                    Kiss him

ITHAMORE

That kiss again, she runs division of my lips. What an eye
she casts on me! It twinkles like a star.

COURTESAN

Come my dear love, let's in and sleep together.

ITHAMORE

Oh that ten thousand nights were put in one, that we might
sleep seven years together afore we wake.   130

---

113 *ream* five hundred sheets (punning on *realm*)
126 *runs division of* plays rapidly upon, as on a musical instrument

---

129 A line of Marlowesque verse, tailing off into bathetic prose, and suiting
the self-parody of Marlowe's style in this scene.

COURTESAN
  Come amorous wag, first banquet and then sleep.

                                            [*Exeunt*]

                    [Act IV, Scene iii]

              Enter BARABAS *reading a letter*

BARABAS
  'Barabas send me three hundred crowns.'
  Plain Barabas: oh that wicked courtesan!
  He was not wont to call me Barabas.
  'Or else I will confess': ay, there it goes:
  But if I get him, *coupe de gorge* for that.   5
  He sent a shaggy tottered staring slave,
  That when he speaks, draws out his grisly beard,
  And winds it twice or thrice about his ear;
  Whose face has been a grind-stone for men's swords,
  His hands are hacked, some fingers cut quite off;   10
  Who when he speaks, grunts like a hog, and looks
  Like one that is employed in catzerie,
  And cross-biting, such a rogue
  As is the husband to a hundred whores:
  And I by him must send three hundred crowns.   15
  Well, my hope is, he will not stay there still;
  And when he comes—Oh that he were but here!

                    Enter PILIA-BORZA

PILIA-BORZA
  Jew, I must ha' more gold.
BARABAS
  Why, want'st thou any of thy tale?
PILIA-BORZA
  No; but three hundred will not serve his turn.   20

131 *wag* youth
  5 *coupe de gorge* (French) '[I'll] cut [his] throat'
  6 *tottered* tattered, ragged
  7 *grisly* fearsome
 12 *in catzerie* i.e. as a pimp and a prostitute's bully, *cf. catso*, IV. i, 20
 13 *cross-biting* cheating
 19 *tale* sum

BARABAS
Not serve his turn, sir?

PILIA-BORZA
No sir; and therefore I must have five hundred more.

BARABAS
I'll rather—

PILIA-BORZA
Oh good words, sir, and send it you were best; see, there's
his letter.   25

BARABAS
Might he not as well come as send? Pray bid him come and
fetch it; what he writes for you, ye shall have straight.

PILIA-BORZA
Ay, and the rest too, or else—

BARABAS [*aside*]
I must make this villain away: – Please you dine with me, sir,
and you shall be most heartily (*aside*) poisoned.   30

PILIA-BORZA
No, god-a-mercy, shall I have these crowns?

BARABAS
I cannot do it, I have lost my keys.

PILIA-BORZA
Oh, if that be all, I can pick ope your locks.

BARABAS
Or climb up to my counting-house window: you know my
meaning.   35

PILIA-BORZA
I know enough, and therefore talk not to me of your
counting-house; the gold, or know Jew it is in my power to
hang thee.

BARABAS [*aside*]
I am betrayed.—
'Tis not five hundred crowns that I esteem,   40
I am not moved at that: this angers me,
That he who knows I love him as myself
Should write in this imperious vein. Why sir,
You know I have no child, and unto whom
Should I leave all but unto Ithamore?   45

PILIA-BORZA
Here's many words but no crowns; the crowns.

27 *what he writes for you* i.e. the bearer's hundred crowns

---

30 *poisoned*. Another of Barabas's characteristic asides in which the un-
expected word is substituted for the expected one, in this case 'welcome'.

BARABAS

Commend me to him, sir, most humbly,
And unto your good mistress as unknown.

PILIA-BORZA

Speak, shall I have 'em, sir?

BARABAS

Sir here they are.   50
[*aside*] Oh that I should part with so much gold!—
Here take 'em, fellow, with as good a will—
[*aside*] As I would see thee hanged; – oh, love stops my
                                                      breath:
Never loved man servant as I do Ithamore.

PILIA-BORZA

I know it, sir.   55

BARABAS

Pray when, sir, shall I see you at my house?

PILIA-BORZA

Soon enough to your cost, sir; fare you well.

                                                 Exit

BARABAS

Nay to thine own cost, villain, if thou com'st.
Was ever Jew tormented as I am?
To have a shag-rag knave to come convey   60
Three hundred crowns, and then five hundred crowns?
Well, I must seek a means to rid 'em all,
And presently: for in his villainy
He will tell all he knows and I shall die for't.
I have it.   65
I will in some disguise go see the slave,
And how the villain revels with my gold.

                                                 Exit

[Act IV, Scene iv]

Enter COURTESAN, ITHAMORE, PILIA-BORZA

COURTESAN

I'll pledge thee, love, and therefore drink it off.

ITHAMORE

Say'st thou me so? Have at it; and do you hear?
                                          [*whispers to her*]

48 *as unknown* as yet unacquainted   60 *come convey* ed. (Q come)
63 *presently* immediately

---

2 *do you hear?* Ithamore's whispered request, of course, is that the
Courtesan shall go to bed with him soon. They have just finished the
banquet.

COURTESAN

Go to, it shall be so.

ITHAMORE

Of that condition I will drink it up; here's to thee.

COURTESAN

Nay, I'll have all or none.   5

ITHAMORE

There, if thou lov'st me do not leave a drop.

COURTESAN

Love thee, fill me three glasses.

ITHAMORE

Three and fifty dozen, I'll pledge thee.

PILIA-BORZA

Knavely spoke, and like a knight at arms.

ITHAMORE

Hey *Rivo Castiliano*, a man's a man.   10

COURTESAN

Now to the Jew.

ITHAMORE

Ha! To the Jew, and send me money you were best.

PILIA-BORZA

What wouldst thou do if he should send thee none?

ITHAMORE

Do nothing; but I know what I know, he's a murderer.

COURTESAN

I had not thought he had been so brave a man.   15

ITHAMORE

You knew Mathias and the Governor's son, he and I killed
'em both, and yet never touched 'em.

PILIA-BORZA

Oh bravely done.

ITHAMORE

I carried the broth that poisoned the nuns, and he and I
– snicle! hand to! fast! – strangled a friar.   20

5 *Courtesan* ed. (Q *Pil.*)
10 *Rivo Castiliano* (pseudo-Spanish slang of drinkers) let the drink
    flow (?)
12 *Ha! To* ed. (Q Ha to)
19–20 *I – snicle! hand to! fast!* – ed. (Q I snicle hand too fast,) 'Snare
    him! Lay your hand to it! Firmly now!' (Kittredge, quoted Spencer)

---

9 *Knavely spoke*. Playing on the sound of the usual phrase 'bravely spoke'
   (*cf.* line 18, 'bravely done'), and the antithesis of 'knave' and 'knight'.
   Applauding Ithamore's valour in thus venturing upon the drink and
   the Courtesan.
12 *Ha! To the Jew*. The Courtesan has ironically proposed the health of
   Barabas as founder of the feast. Ithamore thereupon drinks, and threatens
   the absent Jew as though he were present.

COURTESAN
You two alone.
ITHAMORE
We two, and 'twas never known, nor never shall be for me.
PILIA-BORZA [*aside*]
This shall with me unto the Governor.
COURTESAN [*aside*]
And fit it should: but first let's ha' more gold.
Come gentle Ithamore, lie in my lap.   25
ITHAMORE
Love me little, love me long, let music rumble,
Whilst I in thy incony lap do tumble.

Enter BARABAS *with a lute, disguised*

COURTESAN
A French musician, come let's hear your skill?
BARABAS
Must tuna my lute for sound, twang twang first.
ITHAMORE
Wilt drink Frenchman, here's to thee with a — Pox on this   30
drunken hiccup.
BARABAS
Gramercy, monsieur.
COURTESAN
Prithee, Pilia-Borza, bid the fiddler give me the posy in
his hat there.
PILIA-BORZA
Sirrah, you must give my mistress your posy.   35
BARABAS
A vôtre commandement, madame.
COURTESAN
How sweet, my Ithamore, the flowers smell.
ITHAMORE
Like thy breath, sweetheart, no violet like 'em.
PILIA-BORZA
Foh, methinks they stink like a hollyhock.

27 *incony* ed. (Q *incoomy*) pretty, sweet
36 *A vôtre commandement, madame* (French) At your command,
madam

---

27 *incony*. With an obscene pun; *cf.* Marlowe's translation of Ovid's
Elegies, I.x, 21–1:
    The whore stands to be bought for each man's mony,
    And seekes vild wealth by selling of her Cony.
and Shakespeare, *Love's Labour s Lost*, IV.i, 141.

BARABAS [*aside*]
　　So, now I am revenged upon 'em all.   40
　　The scent thereof was death, I poisoned it.
ITHAMORE
　　Play, fiddler, or I'll cut your cats' guts into chitterlings.
BARABAS
　　Pardonnez moi, be no in tune yet; so now, now all be in.
ITHAMORE
　　Give him a crown, and fill me out more wine.
PILIA-BORZA
　　There's two crowns for thee, play.   45
BARABAS (*aside*)
　　How liberally the villain gives me mine own gold.
PILIA-BORZA
　　Methinks he fingers very well.
BARABAS (*aside*)
　　So did you when you stole my gold.
PILIA-BORZA
　　How swift he runs.
BARABAS (*aside*)
　　You run swifter when you threw my gold out of my window.   50
COURTESAN
　　Musician, hast been in Malta long?
BARABAS
　　Two, three, four month, madame.
ITHAMORE
　　Dost not know a Jew, one Barabas?
BARABAS
　　Very mush, monsieur, you no be his man?
PILIA-BORZA
　　His man?   55
ITHAMORE
　　I scorn the peasant, tell him so.
BARABAS [*aside*]
　　He knows it already.
ITHAMORE
　　'Tis a strange thing of that Jew, he lives upon pickled
　　grasshoppers, and sauced mushrumbs.
BARABAS (*aside*)
　　What a slave's this! The Governor feeds not as I do.   60

42 *chitterlings* sausage-slices
43, 67 *Pardonnez moi* ed. (Q Pardona moy) Excuse me
44 *fill* pour
54 *mush* i.e. much
59 *mushrumbs* mushrooms

ITHAMORE
He never put on clean shirt since he was circumcised.
BARABAS (*aside*)
Oh rascal! I change myself twice a day.
ITHAMORE
The hat he wears, Judas left under the elder when he hanged himself.
BARABAS (*aside*)
'Twas sent me for a present from the Great Cham.   65
PILIA-BORZA
A nasty slave he is; whither now, fiddler?
BARABAS
Pardonnez moi, monsieur, me be no well.

                                                   Exit

PILIA-BORZA
Farewell fiddler. One letter more to the Jew.
COURTESAN
Prithee sweet love, one more, and write it sharp.
ITHAMORE
No, I'll send by word of mouth now; bid him deliver thee a   70
thousand crowns, by the same token, that the nuns loved
rice, that Friar Barnardine slept in his own clothes, any of
'em will do it.
PILIA-BORZA
Let me alone to urge it now I know the meaning.
ITHAMORE
The meaning has a meaning; come let's in: 75
To undo a Jew is charity, and not sin.

                                                   Exeunt

Act V [Scene i]

Enter GOVERNOR, KNIGHTS, MARTIN DEL BOSCO [*and* OFFICERS]
GOVERNOR
Now, gentlemen, betake you to your arms,
And see that Malta be well fortified;
And it behoves you to be resolute;
For Calymath having hovered here so long,
Will win the town, or die before the walls.   5
KNIGHT
And die he shall, for we will never yield.

                    Enter COURTESAN, PILIA-BORZA

65 *Great Cham* Emperor of Tartary
66 *nasty* ed. (Q masty)
67 *me* ed. (Q we)

COURTESAN
Oh bring us to the Governor.

GOVERNOR
Away with her, she is a courtesan.

COURTESAN
Whate'er I am, yet Governor hear me speak;
I bring thee news by whom thy son was slain: 10
Mathias did it not, it was the Jew.

PILIA-BORZA
Who, besides the slaughter of these gentlemen,
Poisoned his own daughter and the nuns,
Strangled a friar, and I know not what
Mischief beside.   15

GOVERNOR
Had we but proof of this.

COURTESAN
Strong proof, my lord, his man's now at my lodging
That was his agent, he'll confess it all.

GOVERNOR
Go fetch him straight.
                                    [*Exeunt* OFFICERS]
             I always feared that Jew.
        [*Enter* OFFICERS *with* BARABAS *and* ITHAMORE]

BARABAS
I'll go alone, dogs do not hale me thus.   20

ITHAMORE
Nor me neither, I cannot out-run you constable, oh my belly.

BARABAS [*aside*]
One dram of powder more had made all sure;
What a damned slave was I!

GOVERNOR
Make fires, heat irons, let the rack be fetched.

KNIGHT
Nay stay, my lord, 't may be he will confess.   25

BARABAS
Confess; what mean you, lords, who should confess?

GOVERNOR
Thou and thy Turk; 'twas you that slew my son.

ITHAMORE
Guilty, my lord, I confess; your son and Mathias
Were both contracted unto Abigail.
'A forged a counterfeit challenge.   30

19 s.d. ed. (Q *Enter Iew, Ithimore*.)
29 *contracted* betrothed
30 *'A forged* ed. (Q Forg'd) he forged

BARABAS

Who carried that challenge?

ITHAMORE

I carried it, I confess, but who writ it? Marry even he that
strangled Barnardine, poisoned the nuns, and his own
daughter.

GOVERNOR

Away with him, his sight is death to me.   35

BARABAS

For what? You men of Malta, hear me speak;
She is a courtesan, and he a thief,
And he my bondman, let me have law,
For none of this can prejudice my life.

GOVERNOR

Once more away with him; you shall have law.   40

BARABAS

Devils do your worst, I'll live in spite of you.
As these have spoke so be it to their souls:
[*aside*] I hope the poisoned flowers will work anon.

[*Exeunt* OFFICERS *with* BARABAS, ITHAMORE, COURTESAN
and PILIA-BORZA]

[*Enter* MATHIAS'S MOTHER]

MOTHER

Was my Mathias murdered by the Jew?
Ferneze, 'twas thy son that murdered him.   45

GOVERNOR

Be patient, gentle madam, it was he,
He forged the daring challenge made them fignt.

MOTHER

Where is the Jew, where is that murderer?

GOVERNOR

In prison till the law has passed on him.

Enter OFFICER

OFFICER

My lord, the courtesan and her man are dead;   50
So is the Turk, and Barabas the Jew.

GOVERNOR

Dead?

31 *Barabas* ed. (Q *Iew.*)
41 *I'll live* ed. (Q I liue)
43 first s.d. ed. (Q *Exit*)
43 second s.d. ed. (Q *Enter Mater.*)
49 *passed on him* sentenced him

OFFICER
Dead, my lord, and here they bring his body.
[Enter OFFICERS, carrying BARABAS as dead]
BOSCO
This sudden death of his is very strange.
GOVERNOR
Wonder not at it, sir, the heavens are just.   55
Their deaths were like their lives, then think not of 'em.
Since they are dead, let them be burièd.
For the Jew's body, throw that o'er the walls,
To be a prey for vultures and wild beasts.
So, now away and fortify the town.   60
                              Exeunt [all except BARABAS]
BARABAS
What, all alone? Well fare sleepy drink.
I'll be revenged on this accursèd town;
For by my means Calymath shall enter in.
I'll help to slay their children and their wives,
To fire the churches, pull their houses down,   65
Take my goods too, and seize upon my lands:
I hope to see the Governor a slave,
And, rowing in a galley, whipped to death.

                Enter CALYMATH, BASSOES, TURKS

CALYMATH
Whom have we there, a spy?
BARABAS
Yes, my good lord, one that can spy a place   70
Where you may enter, and surprise the town:
My name is Barabas; I am a Jew.
CALYMATH
Art thou that Jew whose goods we heard were sold
For tribute-money?

61 *Well fare* blessings on

---

60 *So, now away.* At this point the body of Barabas is supposed thrown
over the walls. This cannot have been performed with any realism.
Dyce's stage-direction reads 'Exeunt all, leaving Barabas on the floor'.
Bennett suggests that the body was carried off-stage, and subsequently
revealed by opening the inner-stage curtains. But more probably the
body was simply tossed forward and allowed to roll towards the front
of the platform. (The Governor's 'So' certainly suggests that his command has just been executed to his satisfaction.) It would then lie
for a moment in full view, an object of anticipatory interest, until
Barabas's rising.

BARABAS

The very same, my lord: 75
And since that time they have hired a slave my man
To accuse me of a thousand villainies:
I was imprisonèd, but scaped their hands.

CALYMATH

Didst break prison?

BARABAS

No, no: 80
I drank of poppy and cold mandrake juice;
And being asleep, belike they thought me dead,
And threw me o'er the walls: so, or how else,
The Jew is here, and rests at your command.

CALYMATH

'Twas bravely done: but tell me, Barabas,   85
Canst thou, as thou reportest, make Malta ours?

BARABAS

Fear not, my lord, for here against the sluice,
The rock is hollow, and of purpose digged,
To make a passage for the running streams
And common channels of the city.   90
Now whilst you give assault unto the walls,
I'll lead five hundred soldiers through the vault,
And rise with them i' th' middle of the town,
Open the gates for you to enter in,
And by this means the city is your own.   95

CALYMATH

If this be true, I'll make thee Governor.

BARABAS

And if it be not true, then let me die.

CALYMATH

Thou'st doomed thyself, assault it presently.

Exeunt

78 *imprisonèd* ed. (Q imprison'd)
87 *sluice* ed. (Q Truce)
90 *channels* drains
98 *doomed* judged
98 *presently* instantly

[Act V, Scene ii]

Alarms. Enter TURKS, BARABAS, [*with*] GOVERNOR *and*
KNIGHTS *prisoners.*

CALYMATH
 Now vail your pride you captive Christians,
 And kneel for mercy to your conquering foe:
 Now where's the hope you had of haughty Spain?
 Ferneze, speak, had it not been much better
 T'have kept thy promise than be thus surprised?   5
GOVERNOR
 What should I say, we are captives and must yield.
CALYMATH
 Ay, villains, you must yield, and under Turkish yokes
 Shall groaning bear the burden of our ire;
 And Barabas, as erst we promised thee,
 For thy desert we make thee Governor;   10
 Use them at thy discretion.
BARABAS
 Thanks, my lord.
GOVERNOR
 Oh fatal day to fall into the hands
 Of such a traitor and unhallowed Jew!
 What greater misery could heaven inflict?   15
CALYMATH
 'Tis our command: and Barabas, we give
 To guard thy person, these our Janizaries:
 Intreat them well, as we have usèd thee.
 And now, brave Bassoes, come, we'll walk about
 The ruined town, and see the wrack we made: 20
 Farewell brave Jew, farewell great Barabas.
       Exeunt [CALYMATH *and* BASSOES]
BARABAS
 May all good fortune follow Calymath.
 And now, as entrance to our safety,
 To prison with the Governor and these
 Captains, his consorts and confederates.   25
GOVERNOR
 Oh villain, heaven will be revenged on thee.
       Exeunt [*all except* BARABAS]

1 *vail* abase	5 *T'have* ed. (Q To)
9 *erst* formerly	10 *thee* ed. (Q the)
17 *Janizaries* Turkish foot-soldiers	18 *Intreat, used* treat, treated
20 *wrack* damage	23 *entrance* the first step

BARABAS
   Away, no more, let him not trouble me.
   Thus hast thou gotten, by thy policy,
   No simple place, no small authority.
   I now am Governor of Malta; true,   30
   But Malta hates me, and in hating me
   My life's in danger, and what boots it thee
   Poor Barabas, to be the Governor,
   When as thy life shall be at their command?
   No, Barabas, this must be looked into;   35
   And since by wrong thou got'st authority,
   Maintain it bravely by firm policy,
   At least unprofitably lose it not:
   For he that liveth in authority,
   And neither gets him friends, nor fills his bags,   40
   Lives like the ass that Aesop speaketh of,
   That labours with a load of bread and wine,
   And leaves it off to snap on thistle tops:
   But Barabas will be more circumspect.
   Begin betimes, occasion's bald behind,   45
   Slip not thine opportunity, for fear too late
   Thou seek'st for much, but canst not compass it.
   Within here!

          Enter GOVERNOR *with a* GUARD

GOVERNOR
   My lord?
BARABAS
   Ay, lord, thus slaves will learn.   50
   Now Governor—Stand by there, wait within—
                       [*Exeunt* GUARD]
   This is the reason that I sent for thee;
   Thou seest thy life, and Malta's happiness,
   Are at my arbitrement; and Barabas
   At his discretion may dispose of both: 55
   Now tell me, Governor, and plainly too,
   What think'st thou shall become of it and thee?
GOVERNOR
   This, Barabas; since things are in thy power,
   I see no reason but of Malta's wrack,

  32 *boots* avails
  45 *occasion* opportunity, time
  54 *arbitrement* disposal, command
  58 *This, Barabas;* ed. (Q This; Barabas,)
  59 *wrack* ruin

Nor hope of thee but extreme cruelty,   60
Nor fear I death, nor will I flatter thee.

BARABAS

Governor, good words, be not so furious;
'Tis not thy life which can avail me aught,
Yet you do live, and live for me you shall;
And as for Malta's ruin, think you not   65
'Twere slender policy for Barabas
To dispossess himself of such a place?
For sith, as once you said, within this isle
In Malta here, that I have got my goods,
And in this city still have had success,   70
And now at length am grown your Governor,
Yourselves shall see it shall not be forgot:
For as a friend not known but in distress,
I'll rear up Malta now remediless.

GOVERNOR

Will Barabas recover Malta's loss?   75
Will Barabas be good to Christians?

BARABAS

What wilt thou give me, Governor, to procure
A dissolution of the slavish bands
Wherein the Turk hath yoked your land and you?
What will you give me if I render you   80
The life of Calymath, surprise his men,
And in an out-house of the city shut
His soldiers, till I have consumed 'em all with fire?
What will you give him that procureth this?

GOVERNOR

Do but bring this to pass which thou pretendest,   85
Deal truly with us as thou intimatest,
And I will send amongst the citizens
And by my letters privately procure
Great sums of money for thy recompense:
Nay more, do this, and live thou Governor still.   90

---

62 *good words* speak mildly   64 *Yet* still
64 *for me* as far as I care
66 *slender policy* small wisdom
68 *sith* since
70 *still* always
73 *not known but in distress* i.e. whose friendship is only discovered
      when you are in distress
74 *now* which is now
75 *recover Malta's loss* recapture Malta
82 *an out-house of the city* a building in the suburbs, outside the walls
85 *thou pretendest* you offer

BARABAS
Nay, do thou this, Ferneze, and be free;
Governor, I enlarge thee, live with me,
Go walk about the city, see thy friends:
Tush, send not letters to 'em, go thyself,
And let me see what money thou canst make;   95
Here is my hand that I'll set Malta free:
And thus we cast it: to a solemn feast
I will invite young Selim-Calymath,
Where be thou present only to perform
One stratagem that I'll impart to thee,   100
Wherein no danger shall betide thy life,
And I will warrant Malta free for ever.

GOVERNOR
Here is my hand, believe me, Barabas,
I will be there, and do as thou desirest;
When is the time?   105

BARABAS
Governor, presently.
For Calymath, when he hath viewed the town,
Will take his leave and sail toward Ottoman.

GOVERNOR
Then will I, Barabas, about this coin,
And bring it with me to thee in the evening.   110

BARABAS
Do so, but fail not; now farewell Ferneze.
                                        [*Exit* GOVERNOR]
And thus far roundly goes the business:
Thus loving neither, will I live with both,
Making a profit of my policy;
And he from whom my most advantage comes,   115
Shall be my friend.
This is the life we Jews are used to lead;
And reason too, for Christians do the like:
Well, now about effecting this device:
First to surprise great Selim's soldiers,   120
And then to make provision for the feast,
That at one instant all things may be done.
My policy detests prevention:
To what event my secret purpose drives,
I know; and they shall witness with their lives.   125
                                        Exit

92 *enlarge* set free   97 *cast* calculate, plan
108 *Ottoman* Turkey   112 *roundly* fairly, well
113 *will I* I determine to   122 *done.* ed. (Q done,)

[Act V, Scene iii]

Enter CALYMATH, BASSOES

CALYMATH

Thus have we viewed the city, seen the sack,
And caused the ruins to be new repaired,
Which with our bombards' shot and basilisks',
We rent in sunder at our entry:
Two lofty turrets that command the town.   5
And now I see the situation,
And how secure this conquered island stands
Invironed with the Mediterranean Sea,
Strong countermured with other petty isles;
And toward Calabria backed by Sicily,   10
Where Syracusian Dionysius reigned;
I wonder how it could be conquered thus.

Enter a MESSENGER

MESSENGER

From Barabas, Malta's Governor, I bring
A message unto mighty Calymath;
Hearing his sovereign was bound for sea,   15
To sail to Turkey, to great Ottoman,
He humbly would intreat your majesty
To come and see his homely citadel,
And banquet with him ere thou leav'st the isle.

CALYMATH

To banquet with him in his citadel?   20

---

1 *sack* destruction, damage
3 *bombards, basilisks* types of cannon (Q Basiliske.)
5 Q places this line between 10 and 11; editors place it after 11
9 *countermured* ed. (Q contermin'd), *cf.* I.ii, 399
11 *Where* ed. (Q When)
12 *thus.* ed. (Q thus?)
20 *citadel?* ed. (Q Citadell,)

---

5 This line was obviously misplaced between 10 and 11, which, with the
  necessary change from 'When' to 'Where', give a continuous sense.
  As Bennett notes, if placed after 11 it remains incoherent. I have
  assumed that it was written marginally in the printer's copy, and have
  therefore ventured to place it after line 4, so that 'two lofty turrets'
  stands in apposition to 'the ruins' and the stop after 'town' closes
  Calymath's first sentence. This first sentence would then refer to
  Malta's fortifications, and the second sentence to its natural defences.

I fear me, messenger, to feast my train
Within a town of war so lately pillaged,
Will be too costly and too troublesome:
Yet would I gladly visit Barabas,
For well has Barabas deserved of us.   25

MESSENGER
Selim, for that, thus saith the Governor,
That he hath in store a pearl so big,
So precious, and withal so orient,
As be it valued but indifferently,
The price thereof will serve to entertain   30
Selim and all his soldiers for a month;
Therefore he humbly would intreat your highness
Not to depart till he has feasted you.

CALYMATH
I cannot feast my men in Malta walls,
Except he place his tables in the streets.   35

MESSENGER
Know, Selim, that there is a monastery
Which standeth as an out-house to the town;
There will he banquet them, but thee at home,
With all thy bassoes and brave followers.

CALYMATH
Well, tell the Governor we grant his suit,   40
We'll in this summer evening feast with him.

MESSENGER
I shall, my lord.

                                        Exit

CALYMATH
And now, bold bassoes, let us to our tents,
And meditate how we may grace us best
To solemnize our Governor's great feast.   45

                                        Exeunt

[Act V, Scene iv]

Enter GOVERNOR, KNIGHTS, [MARTIN] DEL BOSCO

GOVERNOR
In this, my countrymen, be ruled by me,
Have special care that no man sally forth
Till you shall hear a culverin discharged

---

22 *of* by   24 *Barabas*, ed. (Q *Barabas*.)
44 *grace us* equip ourselves   3 *culverin* cannon

By him that bears the linstock, kindled thus;
Then issue out and come to rescue me,   5
For happily I shall be in distress,
Or you releasèd of this servitude.

1 KNIGHT

Rather than thus to live as Turkish thralls,
What will we not adventure?

GOVERNOR

On then, begone.   10

KNIGHTS

Farewell grave Governor.

[Exeunt]

[Act V, Scene v]

Enter [BARABAS] *with a hammer above, very busy; [and*
CARPENTERS]

BARABAS

How stand the cords? How hang these hinges, fast?
Are all the cranes and pulleys sure?

CARPENTER

All fast.

BARABAS

Leave nothing loose, all levelled to my mind.
Why now I see that you have art indeed.   5
There, carpenters, divide that gold amongst you:
Go swill in bowls of sack and muscadine:
Down to the cellar, taste of all my wines.

CARPENTERS

We shall, my lord, and thank you.

Exeunt [CARPENTERS]

BARABAS

And if you like them, drink your fill and die: 10
For so I live, perish may all the world.

4 *linstock* long stick holding a match   6 *happily* haply
3 *Carpenter* ed. (Q *Serv.*)
4 *to my mind* as I would wish
7 *sack and muscadine* wines
11 *so* provided that

---

10 Barabas probably shouts this line after the carpenters–all but the last
   two words. He 'has poisoned the wine to remove the witnesses of his
   crimes' (Bennett). His motive is presumably to prevent information
   from leaking out to the Turkish visitors: but, at the speed with which
   events are now moving, motives are relatively unimportant, and the
   dramatic effect is its own justification.

Now Selim-Calymath return me word
That thou wilt come, and I am satisfied.

Enter MESSENGER

Now sirrah, what, will he come?

MESSENGER

He will; and has commanded all his men   15
To come ashore, and march through Malta streets,
That thou mayst feast them in thy citadel.

BARABAS

Then now are all things as my wish would have 'em,
There wanteth nothing but the Governor's pelf,
And see he brings it.

Enter GOVERNOR

Now, Governor, the sum.   20

GOVERNOR

With free consent a hundred thousand pounds.

BARABAS

Pounds, say'st thou, Governor? Well, since it is no more,
I'll satisfy myself with that; nay, keep it still,
For if I keep not promise, trust not me.
And Governor, now partake my policy: 25
First for his army they are sent before,
Entered the monastery, and underneath
In several places are field-pieces pitched,
Bombards, whole barrels full of gunpowder,
That on the sudden shall dissever it,   30
And batter all the stones about their ears,
Whence none can possibly escape alive:
Now as for Calymath and his consorts,
Here have I made a dainty gallery,
The floor whereof, this cable being cut,   35
Doth fall asunder; so that it doth sink
Into a deep pit past recovery.
Here, hold that knife, and when thou seest he comes,
And with his bassoes shall be blithely set,
A warning-piece shall be shot off from the tower,   40
To give thee knowledge when to cut the cord,
And fire the house; say, will not this be brave?

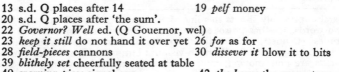

13 s.d. Q places after 14   19 *pelf* money
20 s.d. Q places after 'the sum'.
22 *Governor? Well* ed. (Q Gouernor, wel)
23 *keep it still* do not hand it over yet   26 *for* as for
28 *field-pieces* cannons   30 *dissever it* blow it to bits
39 *blithely set* cheerfully seated at table
40 *warning-piece* signal gun   42 *the house* the monastery

GOVERNOR
Oh excellent! Here, hold thee, Barabas,
I trust thy word, take what I promised thee.
BARABAS
No, Governor, I'll satisfy thee first,   45
Thou shalt not live in doubt of any thing.
Stand close, for here they come. [GOVERNOR *withdraws*.] Why,
                                              is not this
A kingly kind of trade to purchase towns
By treachery, and sell 'em by deceit?
Now tell me, worldlings, underneath the sun,   50
If greater falsehood ever has been done.

Enter CALYMATH *and* BASSOES

CALYMATH
Come, my companion bassoes, see I pray
How busy Barabas is there above
To entertain us in his gallery;
Let us salute him. Save thee, Barabas.   55
BARABAS
Welcome great Calymath.
GOVERNOR [*aside*]
How the slave jeers at him!
BARABAS
Will't please thee, mighty Selim-Calymath,
To ascend our homely stairs?
CALYMATH
Ay, Barabas, come bassoes, attend.   60
GOVERNOR [*coming forward*]
Stay, Calymath;
For I will show thee greater courtesy
Than Barabas would have afforded thee.
KNIGHT [*within*]
Sound a charge there.
    A charge, the cable cut, a cauldron discovered [*into which*
                                              BARABAS *falls*]

50 *worldlings* worldly-minded men   50 *sun* ed. (Q summe)
64 *charge* trumpet signal

64 s.d. *A charge, etc.* A trumpet-signal sounds off-stage, while the Governor
cuts a cord stretched from the gallery to the lower stage (indicated by
Barabas, line 35). He then draws the curtain of the inner-stage, and
Barabas (having staggered backwards through the curtains of the gallery)
is seen in the cauldron. Hunter compares the representation of hell in
mediaeval art (and in a French fifteenth-century miracle play) by a
cauldron, and concludes that Barabas's fall 'has moral meaning as well
as stage excitement'.

[*Enter* KNIGHTS *and* MARTIN DEL BOSCO]

CALYMATH
How now, what means this?   65
BARABAS
Help, help me, Christians, help.
GOVERNOR
See Calymath, this was devised for thee.
CALYMATH
Treason, treason bassoes, fly.
GOVERNOR
No, Selim, do not fly;
See his end first, and fly then if thou canst.   70
BARABAS
Oh help me, Selim, help me, Christians.
Governor, why stand you all so pitiless?
GOVERNOR
Should I in pity of thy plaints or thee,
Accursed Barabas, base Jew, relent?
No, thus I'll see thy treachery repaid,   75
But wish thou hadst behaved thee otherwise.
BARABAS
You will not help me then?
GOVERNOR
No, villain, no.
BARABAS
And villains, know you cannot help me now.
Then Barabas breathe forth thy latest fate,   80
And in the fury of thy torments, strive
To end thy life with resolution:
Know, Governor, 'twas I that slew thy son;
I framed the challenge that did make them meet:
Know, Calymath, I aimed thy overthrow,   85
And had I but escaped this stratagem,
I would have brought confusion on you all,
Damned Christians, dogs, and Turkish infidels;
But now begins the extremity of heat
To pinch me with intolerable pangs: 90
Die life, fly soul, tongue curse thy fill and die.
                                                    [*Dies*]
CALYMATH
Tell me, you Christians, what doth this portend?
GOVERNOR
This train he laid to have intrapped thy life;

74 Q punctuates: Accursed *Barabas*; base Iew relent:
93 *train* plot

Now Selim note the unhallowed deeds of Jews:
Thus he determined to have handled thee, 95
But I have rather chose to save thy life.

CALYMATH

Was this the banquet he prepared for us?
Let's hence, lest further mischief be pretended.

GOVERNOR

Nay, Selim, stay, for since we have thee here,
We will not let thee part so suddenly: 100
Besides, if we should let thee go, all's one,
For with thy galleys could'st thou not get hence,
Without fresh men to rig and furnish them.

CALYMATH

Tush, Governor, take thou no care for that,
My men are all aboard, 105
And do attend my coming there by this.

GOVERNOR

Why, heard'st thou not the trumpet sound a charge?

CALYMATH

Yes, what of that?

GOVERNOR

Why then the house was fired,
Blown up, and all thy soldiers massacred. 110

CALYMATH

Oh monstrous treason!

GOVERNOR

A Jew's courtesy:
For he that did by treason work our fall,
By treason hath delivered thee to us:
Know therefore, till thy father hath made good 115
The ruins done to Malta and to us,
Thou canst not part: for Malta shall be freed,
Or Selim ne'er return to Ottoman.

CALYMATH

Nay rather, Christians, let me go to Turkey,
In person there to mediate your peace; 120
To keep me here will nought advantage you.

GOVERNOR

Content thee, Calymath, here thou must stay,
And live in Malta prisoner; for come all the world

---

98 *pretended* intended
101 *all's one* it's all the same, you are no better off
120 *mediate* ed. (Q meditate)
123 *all* ed. (Q call)

To rescue thee, so will we guard us now,
As sooner shall they drink the ocean dry, 125
Than conquer Malta, or endanger us.
So march away, and let due praise be given
Neither to fate nor fortune, but to heaven.

[Exeunt]

FINIS